Cities in Transition

OTHER VOLUMES IN THE
Conservation of Human Resources Series

Cities in Transition

Changing Job Structures in
Atlanta, Denver, Buffalo, Phoenix,
Columbus (Ohio), Nashville, Charlotte

Thomas M. Stanback, Jr.
Thierry J. Noyelle

Foreword by Eli Ginzberg

LandMark Studies
Allanheld, Osmun — Publishers

To Eli Ginzberg

*In gratitude for his wise counsel, warm support
and infectious enthusiasm.*

ALLANHELD, OSMUN & CO. PUBLISHERS, INC.

Published in the United States of America in 1982
by Allanheld, Osmun & Co. Publishers, Inc.
(A Division of Littlefield, Adams & Company)
81 Adams Drive, Totowa, New Jersey 07512

Library of Congress Cataloging in Publication Data
Stanback, Thomas M.
    Cities in transition.

    (Conservation of human resources series ; 15)
(LandMark studies)
    Bibliography: p.
    1. Labor supply—United States.   2. United States—
Economic conditions—Regional disparities.   3. Income
distribution—United States.   4. Labor mobility—United
States.   5. Labor and laboring classes—United States.
6. White collar workers—United States.   7. Service
industries—United States.   8. Metropolitan areas—
United States.   I. Noyelle, Thierry J.   II. Title.
III. Series.
HD5724.S649   331.11'8'0973   82-1796
ISBN 0-86598-080-2   AACR2

    The material in this publication was prepared under
contract number 21-36-78-33 from the Employment and Training
Administration, U.S. Department of Labor, under the authority
of Title III, Part B of the Comprehensive Employment and
Training Act of 1973. Researchers undertaking such projects
under government sponsorship are encouraged to express freely
their professional judgment. Therefore, points of view and
opinions stated in this document do not necessarily represent
the official position or policy of the Department of Labor.
    Reproduction by the U.S. government in whole or in part is
permitted for any purpose.

82   83   84   /   10   9   8   7   6   5   4   3   2   1

Printed in the United States of America

Contents

Tables

Foreword

The present volume pulls together multiple lines of inquiry with which Professor Thomas Stanback and others at the Conservation of Human Resources Project have been engaged for the last decade and a half. Stanback's first inquiry, *Electronic Data Processing in New York City* (1967), in association with Boris Yavitz, focused on the ways in which New York City's economy absorbed a new technology, electronics, which opened up new business and employment opportunities in the form of computer service firms. In association with Richard Knight, he then spent several years developing a new approach to the metropolitan economy based on a hierarchy of cities analysis, with a focus on job creation and job destruction that was built on a typology of nodal, manufacturing, service (government and medical), and recreational industries, which is used again but with modifications in the present work.

The Metropolitan Economy (1970) was followed by *Suburbanization and the City*,* again in collaboration with Richard Knight, in which Stanback deepened his analysis of the spatial dimensions of changing employment trends, with particular reference to the interactions between central cities and their suburbs. One striking

*Allanheld, Osmun, 1976.

finding is worth recalling: approximately 70 percent of the income of suburbanites in the New York area is city-generated.

Because of the ongoing interest of the Conservation Project in the role of services, Professor Stanback was persuaded to prepare a short monograph focused on services for the purpose of elucidating what theory and trend data might contribute to a deeper understanding of developments on the service front, and that at a minimum would sharpen the questions, even if the answers were not readily forthcoming. *Understanding the Service Economy* (1979) was the product of this effort. Stanback stressed that services should not be studied as totally independent of goods, but rather how the relationships between the two were being altered by changes in technology, organization, and markets.

The present volume represents an extension of this line of inquiry. Its springboard is to examine how seven metropolitan centers in the West, South, and East, with differing industrial compositions, have responded to local, regional, and national forces that have been propelling the U.S. economy increasingly in the direction of services and white collar employment.

Paralleling this study, Stanback, in association with Noyelle and others, undertook two related studies: *Services/The New Economy** and *Economic Transformation in American Cities* (forthcoming).

Since Stanback and Noyelle conclude the present study with a summary chapter, I need do no more than call the reader's attention to it and suggest that it might be a useful place to begin reading. Instead I will select a few themes stressed by the authors that invite additional comment.

I agree fully with their introductory finding that the focus of the U.S. economy's transformation toward services should place more stress on *how* we produce and less on *what* we produce. The importance of this shift in focus is reinforced when one realizes that the value added of "producer services" in independent establishments alone approximates the total value added of all manufacturing output, and that when in-house services of manufacturing establishments are added, the total for producer services is probably even greater, approximately 25 percent.

The associated shift from blue to white collar employment,

---

*Allanheld, Osmun, 1981.

which the authors see as the outcome of more indirect ways of production—more R&D, planning, design, staff specialization—is hard to challenge. They also see the growth of the corporation, with its attendant decentralization of production facilities, as promoting the further build-up of administrative staffs. What they do not address, and I am not sure that it would have been a fruitful area, is the growth of corporate record-keeping and dissemination of information, which may or may not lead to improved decision-making. Many clerks and higher white collar personnel are engaged in the information explosion, but the challenge remains as to how much they contribute to efficiency and profitability.

The authors in their third chapter differentiate sharply between service industries, such as government and distributive firms which have a relatively high proportion of well-paid jobs, and retail and mainly consumer services, which are characterized by a predominance of poorly paid jobs. The producer and nonprofit service firms, they observe, fall in between and are characterized by a dichotomous earnings distribution.

While it is difficult to argue with the authors about their basic reading of the earnings distribution patterns, I suspect that the relative thinness of better paying jobs in many service industries may reflect the relatively early stage of the sector's development.

It is my impression, nothing more, that as the computer industry expands, more and more intermediate level jobs are being developed. I think the same holds true for other producer, nonprofit, and mainly consumer service sectors, from brokerage houses to health care. But I am willing to pay attention to the authors' repeated warning that the opportunities for women and minorities in most of these industries varies from mediocre to bleak, with black males in the most disadvantaged position.

In the last two substantive chapters, 5 and 6, the authors raise a series of tantalizing points. Two examples are the strikingly different patterns of accommodation to the changing economy in the two northern cities, Buffalo and Columbus and second, the authors' reluctance to predict the future of Phoenix and Denver in a too favorable light, especially when comparing these fast-growing but not well-integrated economies to Charlotte, Atlanta, and Nashville, where local, regional, and national factors appear to more closely support each other.

The authors admit that they are clearly worried that the income and occupational mobility channels characteristic of large manufacturing enterprises may not have their counterpart in new service enterprises. If their judgment is correct, they fear that many employees, especially women and minorities, are likely to be permanently trapped in the poorest paid jobs. A recent report by the National Commission for Employment Policy on *Increasing the Earnings of Disadvantaged Women* (1981) provides reinforcement for the authors' concern.

While the authors recognize that education offers an alternative route for mobility, they see difficulties in members of minority groups utilizing this route. Another recent publication of the national Commission for Employment Policy, *Tell Me About Your School* (1980), provides ample evidence for not exaggerating the potential of the educational route.

The authors conclude with the suggestion that we may be moving increasingly toward an unstable dual economy. It is a suggestive formulation but one I am disinclined to accept, at least at this time. Just one counterpoint: white collar employment has historically been more stable, cyclically and secularly, than blue collar.

The authors are modest when it comes to policy recommendations, but they are strong advocates for better data collection and data analysis by government agencies and for more research on the cutting edge of the evolving economy. In these respects I accept and reinforce their plea, for in the absence of expanded knowledge our efforts at reform and improvement will remain hit or miss.

Eli Ginzberg, Director
Conservation of Human Resources
November 1981   Columbia University

Acknowledgments

We wish to thank Bruce Levine of the Bureau of Economic Analysis, U.S. Department of Commerce, for preparing the data of the ten-percent sample of the Social Security Continuous Work History Sample used in this study, and Dr. Marcia Freedman of the Conservation of Human Resources Project for making available data gathered and processed for her own research. Dr. Eli Ginzberg provided encouragement throughout the course of the study. The research assistance of Winny Lin, Robert Watts, and Tom Wong was invaluable.

We are also grateful to the many individuals who helped sharpen our understanding of the seven places covered by this study during field trip meetings or telephone conversations.

Kathy Naughton of the Office of Research and Development, Employment and Training Administration, proved to be very understanding of the difficulties and delays we encountered with the data and provided very helpful comments on a first draft of this manuscript. So did three other readers.

CHAPTER 1

Introduction

This study seeks to identify some of the critical dimensions of change undergone by metropolitan labor markets during the 1970s through a comparative analysis of seven large and medium-sized Standard Metropolitan Statistical Areas (SMSAs): Atlanta, Denver, Buffalo, Phoenix, Columbus (Ohio), Nashville, and Charlotte.

The work is based on two fundamental premises: first, that the U.S. economy has experienced over the past fifteen or twenty years, and to a large extent is still undergoing, a major structural transformation manifested by a disproportionately high growth of many and varied service activities and a rapid white collarization of its labor force within both service and nonservice industries; second, that this transformation has resulted in a concomitant restructuring of the urban system in which the fast-growing services and the rapidly expanding white collar occupations have differentially altered both the industrial composition of metropolitan centers and the nature of work in such places (Chapter 2).

Once these premises are firmly established, the study proceeds by setting forth the record as regards the combined effect of the rise of the services industries and the process of white collarization on the labor force. This is done first for the nation's labor force

(Chapter 3), after which the applicability of some of the findings is discussed for the metropolitan labor markets selected by using a somewhat unusual data base—the 10-percent sample of the Continuous Work History Sample (Chapter 4).*

Having shown, at a first general level of analysis, certain important similarities between local and national characteristics of the service and nonservice industries (Chapter 4), the study continues by identifying some of the differences that may exist among the seven metropolitan labor markets as a result of variations in their economic mission, industry mix, and institutional structure (Chapter 5). The implications of these differences for opportunities for earnings improvements and upward mobility of individual workers in each of these seven labor markets is then evaluated (Chapter 6).

The study concludes by trying to formulate a partial answer to what appears to be a major paradox of the ongoing transformation. The paradox: while the transformation to a service economy seems to have been fruitful in the sense of opening up employment opportunities in large numbers, it appears also to have contributed to creating a more divided labor market structure characterized by a polarization of earnings and by systems of work in which workers at the bottom of the structure face restricted opportunities for advancement.

While not everyone may share the pessimism we express as regards such development, one cannot easily ignore the magnitude of the challenges that society is likely to face as a result of this unfolding paradox. These challenges call for a much better understanding of what is currently changing the functioning of labor markets and of what new kinds of public sector intervention are needed on both the demand and supply side of these markets (Chapter 7).

Because this short study is aimed not as much at offering a large number of new and dramatic empirical findings as at formulating —perhaps more clearly than has been done heretofore—the nature of the employment problems arising out of the growth of services, a few words are necessary to explain the nature of the data analyzed and the importance of the focus on metropolitan labor markets.

It should be noted at the outset that any study of changes in the

*See below and opening paragraphs of Chapter 4 for a discussion of this data base.

occupational matrix of the labor force remains empirically difficult because of the lack of detailed "occupation by industry" data for both the nation and individual SMSAs for years not covered by the decennial census. Since the late 1960s, however, the Bureau of Labor Statistics of the Department of Labor has made available on an annual basis a sample survey of the occupational (but not earnings) structure of the nation's labor force: the *National Industry-Occupational Employment Matrix.* In addition, in the mid-1970s the Department of Commerce, Bureau of the Census, carried out a sample survey, *Survey of Income and Education,* which is fairly comparable in terms of occupational definitions and which provides some information on the earnings structure of the labor force. Although these data are helpful in studying the degree of transformation that has gone on at the national level (Chapter 3), they do not provide information for specific places.

Until very recently the best available source for studying changing earnings characteristics and related work attributes of the labor force in metropolitan labor markets has been the 1-percent sample of the *Continuous Work History Sample* (CWHS) based on Social Security data, but these materials are not suitable for studying medium-size labor markets because of sample size. In Chapters 4 and 6 we make use of a larger, more recent, 10-percent sample of the CWHS (available for two periods 1971–1973 and 1973–1975), which is more adequate in terms of sample size, although it is limited in terms of coverage of the entire workforce, detailed identification of industries, and information regarding earnings distribution.

Several criteria have guided the choice of the seven metropolitan labor markets analyzed in this study. *First,* we have opted for medium to large metropolitan labor markets, rather than the very largest SMSAs, on the grounds that the former economies show greater tendencies toward differentiation and specialization among industrial bases than the latter, which tend to be more alike (see Chapter 2).* *Second,* we have tried to select

---

*In addition, large and middle-sized places have had the least study, while some work has been done on very large SMSAs. For example, see Conservation of Human Resources Project, *The Corporate Headquarters Complex in New York City* (New York: Conservation of Human Resources, 1977); Robert Cohen, "The Internationalization of Capital and U.S. Cities" (PhD. dissertation, New School for Social Research, New York, 1979); Dale L. Hiestand and Dean M. Morse, *Comparative Metropolitan Employment Complexes: New York, Chicago, Los Angeles, Houston, Atlanta* (Montclair: Allanheld, Osmun, 1979).

places with different experiences of transformation to the services, although we do not contend that we have necessarily arrived at the optimal choice. *Third* and last, we have tried to choose places with sharply differing experiences of growth and with rather different regional conditions. The outcome of this process has resulted in the selection of Atlanta, Denver, Buffalo, Phoenix, Columbus (Ohio), Nashville, and Charlotte.

The study of these seven labor markets is structured as follows: Chapter 4 points out and elaborates the general applicability at the local level of the national findings regarding the structure of employment in service and nonservice industries. This discussion, based on an analysis of the 10-percent sample CWHS data secured for the seven places, consists of an examination of the average trends and tendencies found among these seven labor markets. The modified average is the statistical measure used throughout this chapter. By contrast, Chapters 5 and 6 attempt to spell out certain differences among these seven labor markets. Chapter 5 draws on more conventional data on employment by industry and by place (based on the *County Business Patterns*) and on profiles of the corporate-institutional structure of each place derived from various business directories. Chapter 6 displays more of the detailed 10-percent sample CWHS data on a place-by-place basis. Field trips to four of the places (Denver, Phoenix, Columbus, and Charlotte) greatly contributed to double-checking and firming up our understanding of these metropolitan centers.

The analysis carried out in these three chapters is useful in two ways. First, it at least modestly contributes to the discussion of the transformation of metropolitan labor markets, which many researchers and policymakers have come to feel requires greater attention. Second, it supports one of the hypotheses implicit from the presentation offered in Chapter 2, which says that the trends observed when looking at the nation's data should stand out more clearly when they are examined in terms of medium-size metropolitan labor markets. Thus the study of the seven labor markets becomes instrumental in sharpening, in the concluding chapter, the paradox outlined earlier in this introduction.

In the end, this monograph becomes as much a thinkpiece as an empirical analysis. We hope that it will contribute to understanding what we see as a very fundamental policy issue and to pushing research in directions that we feel are in critical need of examination.

Following this introductory chapter, the study is organized as follows: Chapter 2: The Rise of Services and the Urban Transformation; Chapter 3: Labor Market Characteristics in a Service-Oriented Economy: the U.S. Data; Chapter 4: Learning about Metropolitan Labor Markets from the Continuous Work History Sample; Chapter 5: Seven Metropolitan Labor Markets in Transition; Chapter 6: The Impact of the Transformation on Earnings and Mobility; and Chapter 7: The Problems of Work in a Service-Oriented Economy. The harried reader will find in Chapter 7 a summary of the main findings of the study, a broad formulation of the trends to which they seem to be pointing, and some reflections on their policy implications.

CHAPTER 2

The Rise of Services and the Urban Transformation

Students of urban economics have long recognized that employment characteristics and other attributes of cities are influenced by industrial specialization. Seattle differs from New York, New York from Akron—and the differences stem in large measure from variations in economic mission. Wilbur Thompson made this notion explicit a number of years ago in a ringing challenge, "Tell me your industry mix and I will tell your fortune" (Thompson, 1969).

The postwar years have witnessed a major transformation in the industrial structure of the U.S. economy—a transformation widely heralded as the advent of the service economy—with employment in those activities designated as services increasing rapidly in terms of share of total U.S. employment from roughly 57 percent in 1948 to 68 percent in 1978 (see Table 2.1). This transformation, and the largely related shift from blue collar to white collar jobs, have brought with them a major expansion in the employment of women and the appearance of new characteristics relating to working conditions, terms of employment, and the distribution of earnings among workers.

In terms of spatial focus the service transformation has had its major impact on metropolitan economies. Unlike the processes of goods production that have tended to shift to outlying regions, service activities have tended to locate in metropolitan places. Accordingly, growth of services has been strongly associated with the growth of cities, and the economic fortunes of many metropolitan places have been closely tied to their ability to accommodate to the service transformation.

This study looks at a selected number of middle-sized places in an effort to learn more about the kind of special problems and opportunities that are being generated by the changes at play. The present chapter offers an abbreviated overview of the transformation undergone by the American economy and the hierarchy of urban places in the United States in order to set the analysis of these changing metropolitan labor markets in the context of some of the main structural forces that have determined their evolution.

The Shift Toward Services

THE DUAL ROLE OF SERVICES

Fundamental to an understanding of the nature and implications of the rising importance of services is the recognition that such activities play two distinctly different roles in the American economy. On the one hand they are an essential part of the production process (how we produce). On the other, they constitute an important part of final output (what we produce).

Services involved in the processes of production and distribution (in how we produce) may be usefully grouped under two general headings: distributive services and producer services.* *Distributive services* are those activities engaged in distributing goods and services, mostly at the intermediate output level. These services include the industrial classifications transportation, communications, utilities, and wholesale trade. Retailing, because of its close association with the consumer, is classified here as final output (see below). *Producer services* are services that assist user

---

*This classification scheme is similar to that advanced by J. Singlemann in *From Agriculture to Services* (1978). See also Appendix Table 1.

firms in carrying out administrative, developmental, and financial functions or provide similar assistance to public and nonprofit sector institutions. Such firms as finance, insurance, real estate, business services, legal services, and trade associations are classified as producer services.

The reader will recognize that both distributive and producer services are mixed in character, in that firms often provide for the needs of the final consumer as well as business firms and public and nonprofit institutions. It is the *principal* role of the service firm that determines its classification.

Services classified as final output (what we produce) are grouped under the headings *retail trade, mainly consumer services* (hotels, personal services, auto repair services, miscellaneous repair services, motion pictures, amusement and recreation services, private households), *nonprofit services* (health and education services), and *government* (government and government enterprises).* Here again, the conventional industrial classifications do not fit perfectly our classification system since output in some instances is both final and intermediate (e.g., hotels, auto repair service). Nevertheless, we feel justified in classifying according to the most important users.

THE DUAL NATURE OF ECONOMIC TRANSFORMATION:
THE EARLY YEARS

The distinction between *how we produce* and *what we produce* is essential in understanding the major transformations that have been at work in the American economy since the beginning years of its industrialization, as well as the different roles that services have played. During the period dating roughly from the last quarter of the 19th century until the Great Depression, there was a continuous reduction in agricultural employment and a sustained growth in manufacturing. Essential to these changes was

---

*Whether public sector and nonprofit activities are properly classified as final outputs (as they are in conventional, gross national product accounting) is a controversial issue. To a large extent government is engaged in providing for the needs of business firms (a variety of activities, such as police protection, highways, and licensing, contributes largely to the needs of business). Education and health services make possible an educated and healthy workforce, thereby creating human capital—a major input in the productive process. We shall go along with convention in our usage, however.

the growth of retail, distributive, and certain other intermediate services. Retailing, transportation, wholesaling, and to a lesser extent communications, finance, and insurance firms were increasingly called upon to provide a basic service infrastructure. At the same time, agriculture was being mechanized and becoming confined to areas where production was most efficient, and manufacturing was concentrated within the major metropolitan areas and infused with greater and greater amounts of capital for larger scale production. New and more effective means of warehousing, transporting, financing, and distributing goods were continuously being demanded and provided. From 1870 to 1930, TCU (transportation, communications, and utilities) increased its share of employment from 5 to 10 percent of total employment, and wholesale and retail trade, from 6.4 to 12.7 percent (Stanback, et. al. 1981).

During these years, which may be regarded as the era of industrialization, an increasingly urbanized populace was demanding new and different consumer services in the market place and a greater allocation of resources to education. There were gains in the share of employment accounted for by mainly consumer services (despite a continuous decline in domestic services) and education (Stanback, et. al. 1981).

THE POSTWAR TRANSFORMATION

But it is the postwar years that demand our attention here. The past three decades have brought significant changes in the relative importance of services. These transformations are highlighted in employment terms for the period 1948–1977 in Table 2.1. The most important fact shown by the table is that the major shifts in employment to have occurred within the American economy are the result of declines in the importance of agriculture and manufacturing and increases in the role of government, nonprofit, and producer services.

What is most dramatic when contrasted with generally accepted notions is that consumer services, popularly regarded as the most important activities involved in the growth of services in the affluent, late 20th-century society, have not grown rapidly, whereas producer services have played a major role. Also striking is the fact that the distributive services, which played a leading role

Table 2.1 Distribution of Full-Time Equivalent Employees by Industry, 1948 and 1977 (in percentages)

Industry	1948	1977
Agriculture, extractive, and transformative (total)	43.39	31.60
Agriculture	4.31	1.90
Extractive and transformative (total)	39.08	29.70
Mining	2.06	1.02
Construction	4.74	4.58
Manufacturing	32.27	24.10
Services (total)	56.61	68.40
Distributive services (total)	13.54	11.36
Transportation	5.93	3.34
Communication	1.54	1.41
Utilities	1.10	0.92
Wholesale	4.97	5.68
Producer services (total)	6.06	11.96
FIRE	3.49	5.29
Other producer services	2.57	6.67
Retail services (total)	12.57	14.18
Mainly consumer services (total)	7.67	4.99
Hotels and personal services	2.71	2.00
Auto and miscellaneous repair services	0.73	0.86
Motion pictures, amusement, and recreation	0.96	0.85
Private households	3.27	1.27
Nonprofit services (total)	2.61	6.34
Health	1.72	5.19
Education	0.89	1.15
Government (total), of which	14.16	19.57
Public education	2.95	6.44
All domestic industries	100.00	100.00

Source: U.S. Bureau of Economic Analysis, *The National Income and Product Accounts of the United States, 1929-1974* and *Survey of Current Business*, July 1978.

in an earlier era, have declined in terms of share of employment within the economy.

While the recent shifts in employment shares may not always appear very dramatic (obviously, the large scale restructuring of an economy does not occur overnight), they do reflect, at the margin, the fact that we have entered an era in which the bulk of the job increases is in the services as opposed to direct manufacturing, construction, or agricultural production.

Viewed from the GNP side, a number of authors seem to concur that within the private sector, the transformation underway is characterized primarily by an increase in services as intermediate inputs rather than as final outputs (see Denison, 1979; Stanback, 1979; Myers, 1980).*

One must recognize, however, that industrial trends in employment and GNP may differ significantly. For example, manufacturing, agriculture, and certain of the distributive services have shown a much greater tendency to make use of physical capital, incorporating modern technology, than have most of the services, and this is reflected in more rapid improvement in output than employment.† Thus, manufacturing's share of the national product remained roughly the same from 1947 to 1977 (slightly more than 24 percent), and the share attributable to the distributive services increased from 13.4 to 16.5 percent (Table 2.2), although, as we have noted, the shares of employment in both sectors declined. The rise of the producer services is no less dramatic in output than in employment terms, however. For these services the share of GNP rose from 15.5 to 20.1 percent. On the other hand, consumer services declined in importance in output (as well as in employment terms) from 5.5 to 3.1 percent. This decline was accounted for largely by a continued reduction in domestic services. (See Tables 2.1 and 2.2.)

The case of retailing deserves special mention. This important service industry increased its share of employment during the

---

*In Chapter 2 of his book, Stanback notes that the share of final consumer demand for services has indeed not changed much in proportion to total consumption since the late 1950s.

†Extremely controversial questions surround the measurement of output particularly for services, however, and it is by no means clear that differences in productivity gains between goods and services are as great as indicated in the published data (cf. John Myers, 1970).

Table 2.2   Distribution of Gross National Product (measured in 1972 dollars) by Industry, 1947 and 1977 (in percentages)

	1947	1977
Agriculture, extractive and transformative (total)	37.38	32.81
Agriculture	5.57	2.87
Extractive and transformative, of which	31.81	29.94
Manufacturing	24.53	24.18
Services (total)	62.68	66.09
Distributive services	13.36	16.51
Producer services	15.50	20.12
Retail services	11.06	9.89
Mainly consumer services	5.47	3.11
Nonprofit services	2.67	4.04
Government and government enterprises	14.62	12.43
Residual and rest of the world	−0.06	1.10
Gross National Product	100.00	100.00

Source: U.S. Bureau of Economic Analysis, *The National Income and Product Accounts of the United States, 1929-74* and *Survey of Current Business*, July 1978.

period 1948–1977 in spite of a slight decline in its share of GNP. Yet there is ready evidence that there were important reductions in employment through increased customer self-service in certain types of outlets. It would seem, therefore, that the somewhat unexpected rise in relative importance of retail employment must find an explanation in the increasing importance of other types of retail outlets, in which similar labor-saving practices were not present. Under the conditions of rising per capita income, which have obtained until very recent years, it seems likely that we are witnessing here the effects of the growth of small specialty stores that provide merchandise advice and, frequently, special services to customers who have highly individualized requirements (e.g., sporting goods stores, pet shops, hobby shops, gourmet food shops, and health food stores). Such an explanation would be consistent with the discussion presented below relating to consumption trends.

In short, these data do seem to indicate that what has been going on has mostly been a growth in demand for intermediate services. Overall, the share of GNP accounted for by the mostly intermediate services (the distributive and producer services) rose from 29 percent to almost 37 percent of total GNP between 1947 and 1977; that of the mostly final services (retail, consumer, nonprofit, and government) declined from 34 percent to 29 percent.

THE FORCES AT WORK

Behind these postwar transformations lie three major sets of forces: the increasing size of the market, the rise of the modern corporation, and the increased importance of government and the nonprofit services.*

The increasing size of the market. Increase in market size has stimulated both the transformation in how we produce and what we produce. In terms of how we produce, it has opened up opportunities for growth of producer service firms by increasing potential levels of demand sufficient to encourage the birth and growth of specialized services to business and government. These firms, in turn, have enabled user firms to draw upon expertise not readily justifiable or available within their own organizations, thereby making it possible to carry out more complex and larger scale operations.

At the same time, larger markets have changed the marketing strategies and product policy of firms and altered the consumption patterns of individuals. As the national market has grown through increased population and rising per capita income, it has also become broader in scope through breakdown of regional barriers. The result has been the rise of a great national marketplace in which submarkets of individuals with similar tastes have become large enough to warrant exploitation (e.g., submarkets of groups with similar characteristics in terms of ethnic tastes, age, hobbies, and life styles). In reaching out to these new markets, firms have moved toward increased product differentiation and promotion of multiple product lines and have relied increasingly on product differentiation, branding, and aggressive promotion.

---

*For an expanded discussion of these themes, see Thomas M. Stanback, Jr., et al., 1981.

In terms of what we produce, consumers, enjoying higher disposable incomes and facing a wider range of choice, have moved away from older tendencies toward conformity of buying relatively standardized goods purchased by broad segments of society. Instead they have placed greater emphasis on patterns of consumption that stress life style identification and satisfactions of personal taste. Conformity has by no means been eliminated, but it is conformity within a narrower reference group, and conformity which is carried out in terms of a more rapidly changing array of product and service options.

The rise of the large corporation. At center stage among these developments stands the modern national or international corporation. It has both influenced and been influenced by the growth of large markets. On the one hand, it has broken down regional barriers through nationwide promotion and distribution of products and services. On the other, it has provided the only institutional arrangement that is capable of marshalling the vast financial and human resources adequate to engage in the aggressive product development, differentiation, and promotion that these large markets require.

At this point we must call attention to the shift in functional emphasis that has characterized the large corporation. Thus, the routinization of production process (even for relatively highly styled products) through application of modern technology employing computers has simplified the task of production management and permitted the decentralization of plants. Furthermore, the complexities of product development, corporate planning, and finance, and the internal administration of the elaborate organization which is the concomitant of large size, have increased the need for more sophisticated organizational structures and the recruitment of more highly trained professional and executive personnel.* At the same time they have increased the dependence of the corporation on producer services, which in turn has fostered growth and development of higher levels of expertise among producer service firms.

The growth of producer service firms and the increasing impor-

---

*See the rise of the multidivisional and regional organizational structure as discussed by Alfred J. Chandler (1977).

tance of corporate headquarters, divisional administrative, and other stand-alone corporate nonproduction establishments (R&D facilities, distribution centers, accounts receivable processing centers, etc.) are major developments of the postwar era. Since they tend to be located in or around metropolitan centers, they may be expected to influence significantly the character of metropolitan labor markets.

Increased role of government and nonprofit institutions. For the postwar decades taken as a whole, government and nonprofit activities have contributed a major share of employment expansion. This rapid expansion, which has slowed somewhat in recent years, has occurred in a number of ways. At the federal level, government has been heavily committed to enlarging and modernizing the defense establishment (including extensive R&D activity), expanding the scope and size of its public services as well as grant-in-aid programs to states and localities (thereby encouraging them to appropriate additional funds, many of which were directed to increasing public-sector and nonprofit services), and increasing the scope of regulatory and administrative action. At the state and local level, government has been responsive to a widespread demand for service expansion, especially for public education and social welfare, and for attention to the new requirements incident to suburbanization and other population shifts.

The growth of nonprofit institutions has also been of major significance, especially in the areas of health and education. In large measure this process has occurred by means of the expansion of relatively newer institutional arrangements involving both the public and the private sectors. These have provided for the development of what some have called a "grant economy," in which the traditional yardsticks of the private sectors (earnings and profits) have been supplemented by considerations of equity resulting from increased intervention of the public and nonprofit sectors.*

Clearly the expansion of governmental and nonprofit activities has been shaped by a large number of developmental forces, including society's drive for greater equality of opportunity, for a more favorable redistribution of the fruits of postwar growth, and for stronger regulation of the private sector's economy.† While the

*See the work of economist Kenneth Boulding and others.
†See, for instance, Moses Abramovitz (1972).

current concern for the inflationary nature of some of these demands is being translated into some major changes in orientation, it seems reasonable to assume that the government and non-profit sectors will continue to play major roles in the economy.

The Role of Services in Metropolitan Economies

Thus far we have distinguished between major types of services and briefly examined the forces that have influenced their growth. The next question involves the issue of their location within the urban system. We must simply ask: Which services have grown and where?

FACTORS INFLUENCING THE LOCATION OF SERVICES

An initial observation is that goods and services are distinguished largely by the fact that the former can typically be stored and shipped, whereas the latter cannot. Thus service firms tend to locate as close to customers as is feasible, whereas goods-producing firms may respond to a number of factors, such as labor costs, proximity to raw materials or suppliers, and accessibility to broad regional or national markets.

But this does not mean that services are distributed evenly across the urban landscape. Quite the contrary; some services, such as grocery stores and automobile service stations, are virtually ubiquitous while others, such as patent lawyers or large investment banking houses, are found in selective, key cities (often but not always major metropolitan centers) (see Cohen, 1977; Noyelle and Stanback, forthcoming).

The economic factors that govern the location of services include economies of scale in the production processes, extent of demand, and transportation costs (the delivery costs to seller or buyer). Economies of scale dictate the size a firm must attain to compete. For instance, there are few scale economies in a service station, whereas in the operation of a full line department store such economies are of major importance. Thus service stations can operate successfully by selling to limited markets and are sprinkled liberally across the land—in rural areas, small towns, and large cities alike. Department stores, on the other hand, must draw upon larger surrounding areas for their customers.

At the same time levels of population density and costs of transportation affect the geographical scope of market areas. In sparsely populated areas transportation costs may limit the kinds of firms that may operate successfully. Large cities, however, with their dense market areas can support a wide variety of service activities.

These simple notions, though useful, do not suffice to explain the tendency among certain services to be located disproportionately in larger urban places. In addition, the concept of agglomeration economies must be recognized. These economies occur to firms when they can operate in close proximity to certain others. Legal firms may need to be close to banks and to the courts; accounting and advertising firms, to corporate customers; and so on. Not only do firms locate close to others to be near to customers, but also to be near to other sellers or to collaborate with other firms in rendering a joint service.

In this respect, corporate headquarters, divisional offices, and other specialized service installations deserve special attention since their presence explains much of the variation in locational patterns among a number of services. As developmental and administrative functions have become more important, major corporate offices have increasingly been located in and around key cities in proximity to large banks, lawyers, and other producer services. In turn, they have fostered the growth of the latter. This tendency toward agglomeration of producer service firms and corporate offices has been fed by an important recent trend toward the operation of large corporations in the fields of retailing and consumer services (e.g., fast food establishments, department stores, hotels, auto rental agencies, real estate brokers) through franchise or direct ownership arrangements. In short, the increasing importance of headquarters and other installations or large manufacturing and service corporations, operated separately from plants or service outlets and in proximity to producer services, has become a major factor in determining the industrial and employment composition of a substantial number of our larger metropolitan areas.

But agglomeration tendencies are important not simply among producers services and corporate headquarters or divisional offices; they are important also between these and a host of private sector consumer services, public sector, and nonprofit services.

Specialty retail stores, gourmet restaurants, theaters, universities, major hospitals or specialized governmental services tend to locate more frequently in large places because of the larger markets to be served. In turn, corporations and their attendant producer services are drawn to larger places because of the larger support system of consumer and not-for-profit services to be found there.

Thus, it is important to stress the importance of size in the determination of the industrial and employment composition of metropolitan places. Large places are the most logical sites for activities that require very large markets to operate successfully. This is true both because they are, themselves, large markets and because they tend to be logical points of operation from which regional and national markets may be served. In this respect, they tend usually to have better developed communications, airports, and other distributive services.

Moreover, specialization of function must be seen as strongly influenced by size of market. If department stores in general require fairly large cities or towns to operate successfully, specialized department stores must locate in even larger places to survive. Similarly, very specialized legal firms, advertising firms, hospitals, restaurants and hotels are found almost exclusively in the largest places. Their presence, in turn, serves to create stronger agglomerative tendencies in such places than elsewhere.

One must remain careful, however, not to construe too simplistic a relationship among size, agglomeration, and specialization. As we note below, while most of the largest centers have transformed in the recent decades largely by developing sizeable agglomerations of large corporate administrative facilities and attendant producer services, not all large places have followed the same pattern of development, partly for historical reasons and partly because of the influence of regional specialization. To begin to account for some of those differences, however, we must first introduce an additional concept, that of the export specialization of metropolitan places.

EXPORT SPECIALIZATION OF METROPOLITAN PLACES

Economists find it useful to distinguish between export and residentiary economic activities. Residentiary activities are simply those that provide for the needs of those who live and work in the immediate area. Export activities provide directly for the needs of users outside the local area or indirectly by supplying firms engaged in export. They provide streams of income which permit the importing of goods and services from other places.

Without denying the importance and the export nature of distributive (especially wholesaling) and producer (especially financing) services in key cities of the urban hierarchy in earlier times, for decades (since the advance of the era of industrialization) manufacturing constituted the major export industry of most cities. But with the postwar dispersal of production plants to outlying or distant areas and the rising importance of services, it has increasingly been headquarters, producers services, distributive services, nonprofit services, and public sector services that constitute the export base of a large number of large and medium-sized cities.

It is important to recognize the export nature of these service activities. Headquarters provide services to far-flung manufacturing establishments and service outlets. Producer and distributive services provide for the needs of these headquarters and of firms and other customers in surrounding areas and, often, in distant places as well. Likewise, while local governments of cities and towns are essential residentiary activities, state and federal government installations are for the most part export activities, being located in capitals and in selected cities and towns, but performing services for broader areas.*

A major thesis of this study is that metropolitan economies are significantly specialized in terms of their export base, that the terms of their specialization are increasingly defined by different mixes of service (as opposed to nonservice) activities, and that this specialization in export activities influences the occupational characteristics of the workforce and the terms and conditions of employment.

CLASSIFICATION OF METROPOLITAN ECONOMIES

Specialization of metropolitan places does not come about at random. To a large extent, there is a logical ordering of the urban

---

*More generally, many such service activities function as parts of both the export and the local (i.e., residentiary) sector.

system, one which is not a principal concern of this study but which has been analyzed by the authors in connection with an analysis of the American urban system (Noyelle and Stanback, forthcoming). A few remarks on the current structure of the U.S. urban system and its recent transformation are helpful, however, in setting forth the terms of the transformation undergone by the seven SMSAs studied here.

We find it useful to classify metropolitan economies within five broad categories in terms of their export base:

1. nodal places (national, regional, and subregional)
2. functional nodal places
3. government-education places
4. production places (manufacturing, mining, and industrial-military)
5. resort-residential places.

Nodal places are service centers in which exports are concentrated primarily in distributive and producer services and, often, secondarily in other services as well (e.g., nonprofit services, arts, or recreations). Many, but by no means all, are state capitals, and thus are also heavily engaged in delivering public sector services. Usually, the degree of diversification and specialization among nodal centers is a function of their population size and the size of the markets they serve. The presence of corporate headquarters or other administrative installations is of considerable importance in explaining the structure of their economy. Not only do they provide employment for executives and professionals and their supporting technical, clerical, and service staff, but they interact with producer services and, accordingly, are likely to serve as a stimulus for a larger number (and a higher level of specialization) of producer services. The general tendency is that the larger the nodal center, the relatively stronger are the producer services and the relatively weaker are the distributive services (and vice versa). The classification of these nodal centers under three headings—national, regional, and subregional—captures much of the variations that result from market size differences.

Functional nodal centers are places specialized in both manufacturing production and selected service functions of the large corporation: mostly R&D and administration of large industrial divisions. While they can be quite large—many are comparable in size to the regional and subregional centers—they are much more restricted in their service functions than the nodal centers.

Government-education places are for the most part state capitals, seats of large educational institutions, or both.

Production centers include *manufacturing, mining* and *industrial-military* places.* They are characterized by more routine production than that found in functional nodal places, where production is often directly related to new product development and fabrication of higher value-added items. In addition, unlike the nodal or functional nodal places, production centers are singularly weak in attracting administrative or research establishments of industrial corporations.

Finally, *resort-residential* centers include some of the metropolises that out-lie the large national nodal centers, as well as many places that have developed since World War II as resort and retirement centers.

THE IMPACT OF THE SERVICE TRANSFORMATION ON
METROPOLITAN ECONOMIES AND THE
URBAN HIERARCHY

The upshot of the earlier discussion on locational trends among service activities is that the industrial structure of metropolitan economies and, hence, the overall typological configuration of the system of cities are likely to be influenced in a major way by population size.

In order to present in a simplified form the influence of size on metropolitan economies (neglecting, for the moment, variations in functional specialization among similar size places), we examine in Table 2.3 structural tendencies in terms of a three-tier system. The first tier includes the 35 or so largest metropolitan areas with a population larger than one million (size 1 or size 2 SMSAs); the second tier is made up of 100 or so SMSAs with a population range from a quarter to one million (size 3 and size 4 SMSAs); and the third tier includes the 125 smallest SMSAs and other smaller urbanized areas.

For 1976, Table 2.3 shows that places of the first tier were

---

*Industrial-military places are characterized by a large presence of federal government, civilian, and military employees in military bases, shipyards, arsenals, etc.

Table 2.3 Location Quotient of Employment, 1959 and 1976, and Distribution of Employment (in percentages), 1976, among Size Groups of SMSAs

	First-tier SMSAs[a]					
	Size 1 SMSAs			Size 2 SMSAs		
	Location quotient		Employment share	Location quotient		Employment share
	1959	1976	1976	1959	1976	1976
Manufacturing	99.0	90.5	20.7	108.3	89.6	20.5
Distributive services	112.6	112.6	11.7	114.4	112.6	11.7
Corporate headquarter complex	141.6	136.4	20.0	110.3	112.7	16.6
Retail	91.5	90.9	14.5	98.3	106.1	17.0
Consumer services and nonprofit	106.5	105.2	11.4	97.4	106.7	11.6
Government	84.0	86.8	16.9	77.8	89.3	17.4
All industries[b]			100.0			100.0

	Second-tier SMSAs[a]					
	Size 3 SMSAs			Size 4 SMSAs		
	Location quotient		Employment share	Location quotient		Employment share
	1959	1976	1976	1959	1976	1976
Manufacturing	104.5	106.1	24.3	107.7	98.4	22.5
Distributive services	100.4	101.2	10.5	96.7	90.0	9.4
Corporate headquarter complex	94.2	99.1	14.6	88.2	84.3	12.4
Retail	100.9	100.1	16.0	101.5	106.1	17.0
Consumer services and nonprofit	105.2	100.3	10.9	97.7	101.7	11.0
Government	95.8	93.7	18.2	94.3	110.6	21.5
All industries[b]			100.0			100.0

	Third-tier SMSAs and Nonmetro. areas[a]			Total United States	
	Location quotient		Employment share	Employment share	Employment share
	1959	1976	1976	1959	1976
Manufacturing	92.8	113.0	26.0	31.4	22.9
Distributive services	82.7	83.3	8.7	11.8	10.4
Corporate headquarter complex	61.4	59.2	8.7	10.2	14.7
Retail	108.1	105.6	16.9	15.2	16.0
Consumer services and nonprofit	92.5	90.5	9.8	8.0	10.8
Government	128.9	118.7	23.1	16.4	19.5
All industries[b]			100.0	100.0	100.0

[a]Size 1: SMSA population over 2 million; Size 2: SMSA population between 1 and 2 million; Size 3: SMSA population between 0.5 and 1 million; Size 4: SMSA population between 0.25 and 0.5 million; Size 5: SMSA population below 0.25 million. The first tier of the urban system includes all size 1 and size 2 SMSAs; the second tier all size 3 and size 4 SMSAs. The last tier includes all size 5 SMSAs and all remaining nonmetropolitan counties of the nation.

[b]Includes agriculture, mining, and construction not shown above.

Note: The corporate headquarter complex sector combines employment in producer service firms and in headquarters and other administrative units of corporations. Employment in mainly consumer services and nonprofit institutions is not disaggregated.

Source: Thierry J. Noyelle and Thomas M. Stanback, Jr., *Economic Transformation of American Cities*, forthcoming.

characterized by the lowest average percentages of employment in manufacturing and the highest percentages in the corporate head-quarters complex (combined employment of the producers services and of the headquarters and other administrative units of corporations) and in the distributive services. Moreover, the table shows that the shares of employment in the corporate head-quarters complex and in the distributive services tend to decline with size of place, while strong manufacturing employment is a predominant feature among third-tier SMSAs and a selected group of second-tier places. The share of employment in retailing or in the consumer services does not vary significantly with size of place, while the share of employment in government is somewhat larger in the two lower tiers than in the first one.

But Table 2.3 also provides information that sheds light on the transformation that has taken place within the system of cities since the end of the fifties. Location quotients are shown for 1959 and 1976 by industry group and indicate for each size category of SMSAs the ratio of the average share of employment within that industry group in a given size group of SMSA to the share of total U.S. employment accounted for by the same industry, multiplied by 100 to facilitate analysis.*

These data show dramatically the declining relative importance of manufacturing employment and the functional shift toward greater service specialization among many cities of the first two tiers, during the past two decades. In addition, the data point to the growing relative importance of manufacturing activity among centers of the bottom tier. As Table 2.4, to which we now turn our attention, indicates, these changes have resulted in a predominance of nodal-type places among cities of the first tier and a somewhat greater diversity of types among those of the second tier.

Thus, places that make up the first tier are nowadays predominantly classifiable as nodal (Table 2.4), although many were once characterized by their strong manufacturing specialization. Among them we find the principal centers of an earlier era (New York, Chicago, Cleveland, or Columbus) and the newer, major centers of the rapidly growing Sunbelt regions (Houston,

---

*Thus the location quotient for distributive services among size 1 SMSAs in 1976 is 112.5 and is equal to the share, 11.7, for that size group divided by the share, 10.4, for the United States, multiplied by 100.

Table 2.4 Distribution of 140 Largest SMSAs by Population Size and Type, 1976

Type of metropol- itan centers	First- tier SMSAs		Second- tier SMSAs		Representative examples
	Size 1	Size 2	Size 3	Size 4	
Nodal (total)	12	11	9	4	New York, Los Ange- les, Chicago, San Francisco
National	4	–	–	–	
Regional	8	11	–	–	Philadelphia, Boston, Cleveland, Houston, Atlanta, Phoenix, Denver, Columbus
Subregional	–	–	9	4	Jacksonville, Omaha, Richmond, Nashville, Charlotte, DesMoines
Functional nodal	3	3	12	6	Detroit, San Jose, Akron, Dayton, Wilmington, Peoria
Government- Education	1	–	4	15	Washington, Albany, Sacramento, Austin, Harrisburg, Ann Arbor, Lansing
Resort-Residential	1	3	4	4	Nassau-Suffolk, Ana- heim, Riverside, Las Vegas, Orlando, West Palm Beach
Production (total)	–	2	11	35	Buffalo, Worcester,
Manufacturing	–	1	9	19	Gary, Youngstown, Greenville-Spart., York, Reading, Shreveport
Mining	–	–	–	7	Bakersfield, Charleston, W.Va.
Industrial-Military	–	1	2	9	San Diego, Norfolk, Newport News

Note: SMSAs included in this table are all size 1 through size 4 SMSAs (see Table 2.3). Underlines indicate the SMSAs studied in this monograph.
Source: Thierry J. Noyelle and Thomas M. Stanback, Jr., *Economic Transformation of American Cities*, forthcoming.

Atlanta, Phoenix, or Denver). As a group nodal places have undergone a dramatic transformation through decline in shares of employment in manufacturing and increases in shares of employment in corporate complex activities and distributive services (Noyelle and Stanback, forthcoming). Only a few seem to have missed such a well-marked transformation (e.g., Buffalo, see below).

The second tier is much less homogeneous. Of the 104 SMSAs included in this tier in 1976, 58 are service-oriented and 46 are production centers. Of the service-oriented places, 13 are subregional nodal, 18 are functional nodal, 19 are public sector oriented, and the remaining eight show a relatively strong concentration of resort and residentiarylike services.

The experience of transformation of second-tier cities can be thought of, simply, in terms of three fairly distinct groups of SMSAs. The first group—that of the subregional nodal places—is made up of a number of centers with an earlier orientation toward distribution, in which distributive and, to a more limited extent, corporate complex activities have been vigorously developed over the past two decades (for example, Omaha, Richmond, Nashville, or Charlotte). The second group is made up of a sizable number of SMSAs that have remained strongly dominated by their manufacturing base. Some of them, the functional nodal places, appear to have been holding their own by increasingly becoming the host to corporate headquarters, divisional head offices, and research and development establishments, in spite of their earlier strong manufacturing orientation (e.g., Akron, Toledo, Dayton, or New Brunswick). Others, the manufacturing and industrial-military centers, have not been favored by such developments and have experienced serious difficulties in adjusting to the changing economic environment (e.g., Buffalo mentioned above, but also Youngstown, Johnstown, Norfolk or Newport News). The third group includes a number of fast-growing government-education or resort- residential places whose successes are attributable to the rising importance of very specific service functions, such as state government, college and university education, or tourism (e.g., Albany, Austin, Orlando or West Palm Beach).

While Table 2.4 does not present any systematic classification of the smaller, third-tier SMSAs, other research (Stanback and Knight, 1970; Noyelle and Stanback, forthcoming) points to the emergence of a growing number of small-sized manufacturing centers (the beneficiaries of the relocation of production establishments away from the largest centers) as well as specialized service places among this group.

IMPLICATIONS FOR THE SEVEN LABOR MARKETS

The implications of this shorthand presentation of the restructuring of the urban system for the analysis of the seven SMSAs is that similarities and differences in their pattern of transformation may be expected, if only as a result of the constraints to development born out of their past and present positioning within the system of cities. This is no more than the view conventionally held by urban economists that the economic destiny of metropolitan places is in part determined by their functional role in the larger urban system.

Thus Buffalo's recent experience may be expected to differ substantially from that of the six other SMSAs, if only by reason of differences in type: Buffalo is classified here as a manufacturing center, the six others as nodal centers. Manufacturing places have been described, on the basis of our other research (Noyelle and Stanback, forthcoming), as encountering serious difficulties in adjusting to the transition at work, nodal centers as relatively successful in developing producer and distributive services. Likewise, we may expect to find differences among the six nodal SMSAs, if only by virtue of differences in their population size: Atlanta, Columbus, Phoenix, and Denver are regional nodal centers with populations ranging from one to nearly two million; Charlotte and Nashville are subregional nodal centers, with markedly lower populations. As we have indicated earlier, the developmental emphasis among the smaller nodal centers seems to have been placed particularly on the distributive services and somewhat less on the corporate complex; among the larger ones the pattern seems to have been the reverse. Finally, because of similarities in their past experience (heavy emphasis on manufacturing), one might expect to find common features between Buffalo and Columbus, despite probable divergence in their recent experience of development. While, as we shall see, this analysis does not exhaust all possible sources of similarities and divergences among places, it does provide a guideline for the investigation to follow.

Conclusion

In this chapter we have attempted to establish two key propositions that underly much of the following analysis: first, that the U.S. economy is undergoing a major transformation characterized by the rising importance of the service industries and white collar forms of employment; second, that this transformation has resulted in a restructuring of both the urban hierarchy and the economies of many cities.

In analyzing the transformation of the U.S. economy, we have suggested that a six-class typology of the services be used to distinguish among distributive, producer, retailing, consumer, nonprofit, and government services. We have then argued that the transformation can be seen as a dual process of change in *what* the economy produces and in *how* it produces and have identified three major forces of change — the increasing size of the market, the rise of the large corporation, and the increasing role of the public and nonprofit sector.

With this understanding of the transformation at hand, we have then turned our attention to the issue of the transformation of metropolitan economies and the restructuring of the urban hierarchy. Two major observations have been raised: first, that not all services have grown in similar fashion everywhere but that the growth of distributive, producer, and some of the governmental nonprofit services has had the greatest impact on the economy of the largest places; second, that the growth of these selected services accompanied by the declining relative importance of manufacturing among the largest places has had profound implications for the restructuring of the urban hierarchy. Most important for the restructuring of the urban system is the transformation of large and medium-sized metropolitan economies — many of which were once known for their heavy manufacturing specialization — into centers of corporate administration and producer service activities, centers of distribution and other selected service activities. This transformation appears to be in effect in at least six of the seven SMSAs under study here, with indications that the seventh — Buffalo — is experiencing great difficulty in transforming out of its once solid manufacturing specialization. This attempt to explain briefly the positioning of the seven SMSAs in the larger system of cities has been no more than an effort to suggest that the transformation of these economies has not come about at random, but has, to a certain extent, followed a pattern consistent with the logic of the transformation of the overall hierarchy of cities.

CHAPTER 3

Labor Market Characteristics
in a Service-Oriented Economy:
The U.S. Data

Investigation of the characteristics and special problems of individual metropolitan labor markets involved in a transition toward increased service employment calls for analysis of the way such shifts have altered the occupations of workers, the wages they earn in these occupations, and the terms and conditions of their employment.

Ideally, such an investigation should begin by examining for each SMSA the employment in individual occupational groups within the various industrial categories. We need to know the employment composition, its special attributes, and the way it is changing.

Unfortunately, investigation on a place-by-place basis is restricted by data limitations, especially as regards occupation and earnings. Considerable detail is available on a special survey basis for the nation for selected years, however, the most recent of which is 1975.* This chapter makes use of such data to shed light

---

*U.S. Bureau of the Census (1975). The analysis presented in this chapter also makes use of less detailed data provided in U.S. Bureau of Labor Statistics (1960, 1967, 1970, 1976).

on special characteristics of employment, particularly within the various service industries, to record occupational shifts within both the service and the nonservice industries and to assess recent changes and prospects for future developments. In Chapter 4, we assess the applicability of these findings to employment in given industrial categories at the SMSA level.

Occupational and Earnings
Characteristics of Service Industries

The growth of service employment has been strongly associated with what we typically call white collar (professional, technical, clerical, and sales occupations) and "service worker" jobs, yet the services vary widely in terms of the importance of individual occupations (Table 3.1).* For example, professionals account for 36 percent of employment in the nonprofit services (13 percent in health, 51 percent in education) but only 1 percent in retailing. Managerial jobs are relatively important in distributive services, retailing, and producers services, and much less important in the consumer and nonprofit services. Office clericals make up 21 percent of employment in producers services, 3 percent in consumers services. Service workers account for over 40 percent of the employment in the consumer services, close to a quarter of employees in retail and the nonprofit services, and much less anywhere else.

These differences in occupational composition are of major significance for understanding the nature of employment at the industry level, because occupations themselves vary sharply in terms of training and/or experience required and wages and salaries paid. The extent of wage differentials among occupations is clearly indicated in Table 3.2. For the U.S. economy as a whole, average annual earnings of professionals are more than twice as great as for office clericals and almost four times as great as for service workers. In general, these differentials in earnings

---

*The occupational classification *service worker* must be distinguished from the generic term, which simply refers to those employed in the services. The occupational classification includes, for example, cooks and housekeepers, cleaning workers, food service workers, and health service workers.

Table 3.1 Distribution of Employment among Occupations, for Each Industry and for Total United States, 1975 (in percentages)

	Professionals	Technicians	Managers	Office clericals	Nonoffice clericals	Sales workers	Craftsmen	Operatives	Service workers	Laborers
All industry (total US)	10.3	6.9	13.6	8.7	8.2	6.0	11.7	15.0	13.3	6.4
Construction	2.5	1.5	14.0	3.9	1.7	0.3	53.9	7.0	0.3	14.9
Manufacturing	5.4	5.2	11.5	6.2	5.1	2.8	14.9	42.2	1.9	5.0
Distributive services	3.3	3.5	17.0	9.7	11.6	9.5	15.2	21.3	2.0	7.0
TCU	3.8	5.0	12.4	7.0	14.3	0.6	20.5	26.3	2.8	7.4
Wholesale	2.5	1.3	23.6	13.5	7.7	22.4	7.5	14.2	1.0	6.3
Retail	1.1	0.9	18.6	4.8	11.6	18.0	8.0	6.7	24.8	5.4
Producer services	13.5	9.0	17.3	21.3	12.8	11.7	2.6	2.2	8.2	1.5
FIRE	5.2	5.6	21.6	22.7	16.9	18.8	1.9	0.4	5.4	1.5
Corporate services	24.6	13.5	11.6	19.4	7.3	2.2	3.4	4.7	11.9	1.4
Consumers services	0.5	7.2	7.4	3.0	4.2	0.9	13.8	11.7	44.0	7.3
Nonprofit services	36.0	12.9	4.0	11.6	6.3	0.2	2.0	1.1	24.8	1.0
Health	12.9	24.2	4.4	12.8	3.9	0.1	2.2	1.7	37.1	0.7
Education	51.0	5.7	3.7	10.8	7.9	0.2	1.9	0.8	16.9	1.2
Public administration	10.2	25.1	12.0	15.2	18.3	0.1	7.2	2.0	6.5	3.7

Note: Each row sums to 100 percent.

Source: U.S. Bureau of the Census, *Survey of Income and Education,* 1976.

Table 3.2 Relative Level of Average Annual Earnings for Each Industry-Occupational Subgroup with Industries Ranked for Each Occupation, 1975

Industry	Professionals	Technicians	Managers	Office clericals	Nonoffice clericals	Sales workers	Craftsmen	Operatives	Service workers	Laborers	Average rank[a]
All industry (total US)	1.62	1.25	1.48	0.73	0.78	0.91	1.17	0.88	0.44	0.57	
Construction	1.93	1.46	1.54	0.67	1.37	1.11	1.07	1.06	0.36	0.68	5.6
(rank)	6	5	7	7	1	5	7	3	9	5	
Manufacturing	2.02	1.63	1.87	0.87	1.02	1.02	1.30	0.87	0.33	0.84	3.0
(rank)	5	2	2	2	4	6	2	5	10	2	
Distributive services	2.04	1.77	1.79	0.80	1.07	1.64	1.49	1.12	0.36	0.83	
TCU	2.05	1.82	1.93	0.93	1.15	1.42	1.55	1.21	0.97	0.90	1.4
(rank)	3	1	1	1	3	2	1	1	1	1	
Wholesale	2.04	1.52	1.69	0.70	0.85	1.65	1.23	0.88	0.39	0.71	4.4
(rank)	4	4	4	5	5	1	5	4	8	4	
Retail	1.36	0.81	1.14	0.61	0.45	0.52	0.97	0.58	0.34	0.47	9.6
(rank)	10	9	11	9	10	10	9	10	10	8	
Producer services	2.11	1.27	1.53	0.70	0.70	1.36	1.13	0.63	0.59	0.44	
FIRE	1.88	1.36	1.59	0.71	0.73	1.38	1.05	0.86	0.63	0.41	6.1
(rank)	7	6	6	4	6	3	8	6	3	10	
Corporate services	2.18	1.23	1.39	0.70	0.60	1.20	1.19	0.61	0.57	0.49	6.3
(rank)	2	7	8	6	8	4	6	9	4	7	
Consumer services	1.55	0.67	1.23	0.56	0.47	0.66	0.85	0.64	0.29	0.22	10.1
(rank)	9	11	10	11	9	9	11	8	11	11	
Nonprofit services	1.41	0.90	1.48	0.63	0.49	0.87	1.06	0.61	0.51	0.52	
Health	2.20	0.97	1.61	0.67	0.67	0.47	1.24	0.66	0.57	0.68	6.0
(rank)	1	8	5	7	7	11	4	7	5	5	
Education	1.28	0.69	1.37	0.61	0.44	0.99	0.92	0.55	0.43	0.46	9.5
(rank)	8	10	9	9	11	7	10	11	7	9	
Public administration	1.85	1.58	1.76	0.87	1.22	0.89	1.28	1.14	0.74	0.81	3.4
(rank)	8	3	3	3	2	8	3	2	3	3	

a Average rank of occupational earning indexes for each industry group.

Note: Annual earnings have been converted to indexes by normalizing them to the U.S. average earning for all occupation–all industry. Normalized average earnings for the U.S. is thus equal to 1.0. (Average earnings for all occupation–all industry for the U.S. was $8,610 in 1975.) Numbers under the indexes indicate rankings within each occupation, from the highest (#1) to the lowest (#11).

Source: U.S. Bureau of the Census, *Survey of Income and Education,* 1976.

obtain in relative terms within each industry, with the result that average earnings in given industries are strongly influenced by the way in which employment is distributed among occupations.

Nevertheless, differences in occupational composition explain only a part of the differences in average earnings among the service industrial groups. Some industries pay relatively well across occupations, others relatively poorly. Again, this is readily seen in Table 3.2, where average earnings in each of the various occupations are ranked separately among industry groupings, including manufacturing and construction. When ranks of occupations are compared within a given industry they are found to vary little in most instances, although there are a few important exceptions, for instance professionals in health and corporate services. The relatively low rankings of earnings among occupations in educational services, it should be noted, are due in considerable measure to the part-year nature of employment for many in the educational system.

Just how the combined effect of these tendencies works out in terms of earnings distribution of each of the industry groups is summarized in Table 3.3, which shows for each industry the percentage of employment falling within each of five broad income classes. The earnings profiles of the various industry groups vary sharply. Consumer services and retailing are essentially low paying industries, not only because earnings are relatively low across occupations (see Table 3.2) but because these service groups are heavily weighted with low-earnings occupations (see Table 3.1). Distributive services and public administration, on the other hand, are characterized by few poorly paid jobs. For producer and nonprofit services, the distribution shows concentrations of employment in both well and poorly paid employment. For the services taken as a whole, the important observation is that there tend to be heavy concentrations of employment in better-than-average and in poorer-than-average jobs. In contrast, in manufacturing and construction the distributions are more heavily weighted toward medium and above-average income jobs.

The foregoing analysis suggests much about the significance of growing service employment in individual metropolitan economies. The shift to services has been a shift to activities with occupational and earnings characteristics that differ sharply from

Table 3.3   Distribution of Employment among Earnings Classes for Each Industry and for Total United States, 1975 (in percentages)

	Earning classes [a]				
	1.60 and above	1.60 to 1.20	1.20 to 0.80	0.80 to 0.40	0.40 and below
All industry (total US) [b]	12.0	22.2	27.8	28.4	9.6
Construction	2.5	17.2	61.1	18.8	0.3
Manufacturing	20.4	17.4	45.0	17.2	–
Distributive services	32.2	27.8	30.3	9.3	0.4
TCU	20.9	41.0	36.1	2.0	–
Wholesale	48.5	8.8	21.9	19.8	1.0
Retail	–	7.1	32.9	57.1	2.9
Producer services	13.5	38.0	2.8	45.7	–
FIRE	5.2	46.0	2.3	46.5	–
Corporate services	24.6	27.3	3.4	44.7	–
Consumer services	–	4.1	13.7	16.8	65.4
Nonprofit services	6.8	34.1	10.7	48.4	–
Health	17.3	2.3	24.2	56.3	–
Education	–	54.6	2.1	43.3	–
Public administration	22.1	50.6	20.9	6.4	–

[a] Earning class intervals make use of earning indexes in which the index of the 1975 average earnings for all industry is equal to 1.0 (same as in Table 3.2).
[b] Each line sums up to 100 percent.
Source: U.S. Bureau of the Census, *Survey of Income and Education*, 1976.

those obtaining in goods-producing activities, with the individual services differing significantly among themselves. Those places with relatively large proportions of employment in the more favored service industries may be expected to fare better than those with major shares of employment in the less favored.

Changes in Occupations within the Service and Nonservice Industries

While the above analysis, based on the most recent year (1975) for which industry occupational data are available, is generally applicable to the beginning of the eighties, it is important to recognize that the more recent years have seen significant changes in occupational characteristics of employment and that such changes are likely to continue.

Table 3.4 indicates the extent to which employment in given occupations has grown more rapidly or less rapidly than overall employment in their respective service or nonservice industries during the seventies (1970–1976) and the sixties (1960–1967). Employment changes are presented for each occupation on both a hypothetical and actual basis, the hypothetical calculation indicating employment changes that would have occurred if occupational composition (i.e., the share of employment accounted for by each occupation) in individual industries had remained the same.* The actual net changes show the recorded growth or decline in employment in each occupation and reflect both industry growth and changes in the relative importance of given occupations.

The difference between the two sets of changes is labelled "occupational shift" and measures the extent to which actual occupational changes exceeded or failed to attain the levels that would have been expected had there been no change in occupational composition within the various industry groups.

The results for the 1970s are extremely interesting. The shift estimates for the nonservice industries, which are dominated by manufacturing, are the most readily interpreted. We observe a substantial trend toward employment of professionals, technicians, and managers (executives) and away from operatives, laborers, and service workers, indicating a movement toward greater emphasis on administrative and developmental functions within the corporate organization of the sort discussed in Chapter 2. An intriguing finding is that clericals declined slightly in relative importance, reversing a trend toward relatively more rapid growth in employment of clerical workers in the sixties (1960–1967) and suggesting that new forces — very likely the new office technology — are beginning to be felt.

The shift measures for the service industries in Table 3.4 show a similar trend toward increased employment of technicians and managers, which, as detailed analysis (not shown) indicates,

---

*The hypothetical calculation also assumes that the sex composition within each occupation in each industry remains unchanged.

Table 3.4   Analysis of Employment Change by Occupation for Service and Nonservice Industries, 1960 to 1967 and 1970 to 1976

Occupation	1960–1967		
	Hypothetical change	Actual change	"Occupational shift" gain (loss)
		Service industries	
Total	7,486,945	7,486,945	0
Professional	1,797,631	2,199,072	401,441
Technical	706,609	780,785	74,176
Manager	822,576	467,817	−354,759
Office clerical	691,559	605,205	86,354
Nonoffice clerical	908,726	1,080,542	171,816
Sales workers	399,778	262,719	−137,059
Craftsmen	297,305	457,230	159,925
Operatives	368,426	436,953	68,527
Service workers	1,337,296	1,094,843	−242,453
Laborers	157,039	101,779	− 55,260
		Nonservice industries	
Total	1,107,006	1,107,006	0
Professional	112,635	225,407	112,772
Technical	83,683	112,996	29,313
Manager	1,248,928	−1,391,991	−143,063
Office clerical	121,133	163,548	42,415
Nonoffice clerical	193,243	197,501	4,258
Sales workers	68,786	31,398	− 37,388
Craftsmen	504,283	503,773	−510
Operatives	1,049,720	1,429,580	379,850
Service workers	44,569	− 29,850	− 74,419
Laborers	177,882	− 135,356	−313,238

Source: U.S. Bureau of Labor Statistics, *Tomorrow's Manpower Needs, National Industry-Occupational Matrix* (Microdata for 1960, 1967, 1970, and 1976).

characterizes virtually every branch of the services. The negative shift in professionals is largely a reflection of retrenchment in the employment of teachers in educational services, since most other service industries show slight positive shifts. Overall, as among the nonservice industries, there appears to have been a general

Table 3.4 (continued)

Occupation	1970-1976		
	Hypothetical change	Actual change	"Occupational shift" gain (loss)
		Service industries	
Total	8,658,605	8,658,605	0
Professional	1,490,889	1,179,655	−311,234
Technical	753,897	1,258,142	504,245
Manager	960,953	1,444,876	483,923
Office clerical	1,055,177	967,857	− 87,320
Nonoffice clerical	797,616	828,484	30,868
Sales workers	601,705	475,599	−126,106
Craftsmen	366,780	520,326	153,546
Operatives	338,959	263,526	− 75,433
Service workers	2,094,782	1,463,281	−631,501
Laborers	197,847	256,859	59,012
		Nonservice industries	
Total	181,705	181,705	0
Professional	2,693	85,651	82,958
Technical	− 7,237	104,123	111,360
Manager	35,771	133,470	97,699
Office clerical	− 1,635	− 23,651	− 22,016
Nonoffice clerical	− 10,862	− 57,978	− 47,116
Sales workers	− 7,952	7,316	15,268
Craftsmen	191,859	265,452	73,593
Operatives	− 82,570	− 201,419	−118,849
Service workers	− 3,281	− 68,368	− 65,087
Laborers	64,919	− 62,891	−127,810

tendency throughout the services to build up administrative and technical staffs.

The implication of the shift measures for changes in clerical employment in the services is less clear than for the nonservice industries. Detailed analysis indicates strong relative gains in retailing (partly because of the rise in the number of cashiers—classified as nonoffice clericals—in self-service outlets: super-markets, department stores, etc.), consumer services, and non-profit services and indicates relative losses (mostly office clericals) in the remaining services. The implication would seem to be that there is a trend afoot toward at least a leveling off in the employ-ment of office clerical workers in the services in the years ahead (for reasons similar to those hypothesized in the case of the nonservice industries).

The substantial negative shift in the occupational classification *service worker* is largely accounted for by the sharp decline in domestic servants in the consumer services industrial group. It is probable that it is also due to some extent to reduction in the use of service workers through application of labor-saving equipment or changing operational procedures.

The Impact of Employment Growth in Services on the Distribution of Earnings

Given the occupational and earnings characteristics of the services that have been observed, what has been the impact of services growth on the composition of earnings? Table 3.5 sets forth in relative terms the estimated distribution of workers within earn-ings categories for the total labor force in 1960 and 1975 (the last year for which earnings estimates are available). The distribution of wage earners in both 1960 and 1975 assumes the same average (1975) earnings in each industry-occupational cell for both years. Further, earnings in each industry-occupational cell in the year 1975 are normalized against average 1975 earnings for the United States. These normalized earnings are then used for distributing wage earners in both years. The result of using this procedure is that the changes in earnings distribution between the two reflects only the effects of changing industry-occupational mix.

Between 1960 and 1975, we observe a significant change in the distribution of the total labor force, which has resulted from the rise of service employment and the internal occupational shifts that have occurred within both the nonservices and the services sectors. The shares of employment in the earnings classes 1.20 and above (120 percent or more of average earnings) have risen

Table 3.5 1960 and 1975 Distribution of Total U.S. Labor Force among Earnings Classes and Distribution of 1960–1975 Job Increases in the Services

Earnings classes	Distribution of total U.S. labor force (percentages)[a]		1960–1975 job increases in services[b]	
	1960	1975	Numbers of jobs (,000)	Percentage
1.60 and above	10.9 ⎤ 31.6	12.0 ⎤ 34.2	1,947	9.5 ⎤ 35.0
1.59 to 1.20	20.7 ⎦	22.2 ⎦	5,224	25.5 ⎦
1.19 to .80	35.9	27.8	2,311	11.3
.79 to .40	24.1 ⎤ 32.5	28.4 ⎤ 38.0	9,205	44.9 ⎤ 53.8
.39 and below	8.4 ⎦	9.6 ⎦	1,829	8.9 ⎦
Total	100.0	100.0	20,516	100.0

[a] Excludes Agriculture, Mining, and Public Administration.
[b] TCU, Wholesale, Retail, FIRE, Corporate Services, Consumer Services and Non-profit.
Source: Based on U.S. Bureau of the Census, *Survey of Income and Education* (for 1975) and U.S. Bureau of Labor Statistics, *Tomorrow's Manpower Needs, National Industry-Occupational Matrix* (for 1960).

by 2.6 percentage points; the share accounted for by employment in the .80 to 1.19 class has declined by 8.1 percentage points; and the share in the classes below .80 has increased by 5.5 percentage points.

Analysis of job increases by relative income group (columns 3 and 4) shows dramatically the way in which changes in service employment alone have affected the distribution of earnings. Between 1960 and 1975 the industry-occupational subgroups of services with earnings levels 120 percent or more of the national average accounted for 35 percent of all gains in services; subgroups with earnings levels below 80 percent accounted for 53.8 percent. Subgroups with earnings levels ranging from 80 to 120 percent were responsible for a mere 11.3 percent. In short, the growth of services in recent times has moved the economy toward a greater inequality in earnings.

Service Employment of Women
and Minorities

FEMALE EMPLOYMENT

Perhaps one of the most important dimensions of labor market transformation in the recent decades has been the rise of female participation in the labor force. In less than two decades (1965–1980), women's participation rates went up from 35 percent to well over 50 percent, while male participation declined slightly from 82 percent to 78 percent (U.S. Bureau of Census, 1980). The sharp increase in female employment has been largely associated with the growth of the services. During the decade of the sixties, 81 percent of all increases in women's jobs were in the services. In 1975, 49 percent of jobs in the service industries were held by women, and 24 percent of jobs in the nonservice categories.

But women have by no means gained equal access to all types of service jobs. Table 3.6, which presents the percentage of female employment in each industry-occupational subgroup for 1975, indicates that women dominate certain types of employment but find relatively few jobs in others. For example, women account for a major share of both office and nonoffice clerical jobs in almost every industry; of technicians jobs in retail, health, and education; and of service worker jobs in those industries in which this occupation is important (retail, consumer services, and nonprofit services). In general, they tend to be confined largely to low-paid jobs, regardless of whether they are in service or nonservice industries.

Given such variation in the percentage of female employment among industry-occupational subgroups, it is not surprising that industries differ sharply in terms of the importance of women's jobs. For example, the TCU (transportation, communications, utilities) grouping shows only 22 percent female employment, while health services shows 75 percent, and educational services, 61 percent. In general, among the services, female employment is highest among nonprofit services, retailing, FIRE, and consumer services, and lowest in the distributive services and in public administration. Manufacturing and construction are characterized by relatively low levels of female employment. If detailed

Table 3.6 Female Employment Share in Each Industry-Occupational Subgroup in the United States, 1975 (in percentages)

	Professionals	Technicians	Managers	Office clericals	Nonoffice clericals	Sales workers	Craftsmen	Operatives	Service workers	Laborers	All occupations
All industry (total US)	39.1	40.6	18.7	92.9	64.3	41.2	4.4	32.0	64.4	11.0	39.7
Construction	9.4	3.9	3.3	90.0	18.5	13.7	0.4	0.3	26.4	1.3	5.2
Manufacturing	13.2	15.8	10.2	91.6	38.9	15.8	5.7	40.2	16.4	13.7	29.6
Distributive services	11.0	17.3	10.1	90.0	55.5	7.8	2.8	11.9	34.8	4.4	22.5
TCU	11.1	17.5	10.1	85.6	60.0	36.6	2.4	10.2	36.9	1.2	21.6
Wholesale	10.5	16.2	10.2	93.3	43.3	6.6	4.0	16.6	26.0	9.7	23.9
Retail	28.8	53.1	26.3	94.5	81.2	60.9	10.9	20.2	63.3	13.7	49.3
Producer services	17.7	30.7	32.0	92.5	76.8	28.0	8.9	35.3	24.6	4.7	46.6
FIRE	26.7	40.9	32.3	92.8	80.9	27.3	7.2	0.3	26.0	6.6	52.2
Corporate services	15.2	25.0	31.3	92.1	64.2	34.9	10.2	39.2	23.8	2.0	39.1
Consumer services	25.1	34.0	19.4	94.3	70.5	45.1	3.7	33.8	79.6	5.5	50.2
Nonprofit services	52.6	80.5	47.0	96.5	82.6	46.0	12.2	49.0	72.4	13.7	66.6
Health	27.4	88.2	50.4	97.2	85.8	67.5	10.2	60.6	81.9	29.1	74.7
Education	56.7	59.7	44.3	96.0	81.6	40.0	13.7	33.5	58.9	7.6	61.4
Public administration	24.7	13.5	23.0	89.0	38.9	44.6	1.7	9.2	33.4	67.0	32.0

Source: U.S. Bureau of the Census, Survey of Income and Education, 1976.

Table 3.7 Nonwhite Employment Share in Each Service Industry-Occupational Subgroup in the United States, 1975 (in percentages)

	Professionals	Technicians	Managers	Office clericals	Nonoffice clericals	Sales workers	Craftsmen	Operatives	Service workers	Laborers
Truck and Warehousing								13		31
Transportation								16	23	34
Communications				14	16	20			36	42
Utilities								24	24	32
Wholesale					13			17	21	19
Retail, nondurable								12	19	
Retail, durable		16						17	27	17
FIRE							20	24	27	
Producer services									23	24
Health services					15			29	21	21
Education, Welfare	10[a]				13		12	23	24	16
Restaurants, Hotels					12	14	12	18	13	22
Personal, Repair services		13	12					23	23	15
Public administration					16		14	38	28	23

[a]Shown only for purposes of reference in the text.

Note: Only industry-occupational subgroupings with 12 percent or more nonwhite employment are shown.

Source: U.S. Bureau of the Census, *Survey of Income and Education*, 1976.

manufacturing classification were shown, however, there would no doubt be considerable variation. Female employment in apparel production, for example, would be expected to be high.

NONWHITE EMPLOYMENT

Minorities of both sexes have found restricted access to employment in the services. Table 3.7 indicates for services those industry-occupational cells in which nonwhite employment was 12 percent or greater in 1975. (The share of nonwhite workers in the labor force in 1975 was 11.5 percent.) We observe that minority employment (both sexes) tends to be confined to certain occupations — largely operatives, laborers, and service workers — although nonwhites account for 12 percent or more of employment among nonoffice clericals in close to half of the service industry categories.

The greater success of nonwhites in finding employment in certain services — e.g., restaurants, education services or public administration — is apparent, but even here they are poorly represented in a number of occupations. Only in educational services is employment of minorities as professionals as high as 10 percent.

Even more worrisome is the fact that while participation rates for black and other minority females improved slightly during the 1965–1980 period, from 48 percent to just over 50 percent, that of black and other minority males decreased substantially during the same period, from over 78 percent to under 69 percent (U.S. Bureau of Census, 1980). Their restricted access to employment in the service industries, discussed above, may be one element of an explanation, although one would suspect that this is only part of a broader problem.

Special Characteristics of Service Employment

JOB SHELTERING AND INTERNAL LABOR MARKETS

In discussing sheltering, Marcia Freedman (1976, p. 113) has written:

The term suggests different but related themes. First is the relationship of job protection mechanisms to the determination of annual earnings, where 'shelter' implies retreat from competition and the sum of arrangements that give workers strong claims to their jobs. Second, 'shelter' signifies a search for protection against adversity and the mitigation of the effects of unemployment, disability, illness and old age.

In practice, sheltering is most likely to occur where workers are protected through union membership, licensing, or accreditation, or by virtue of employment in large organizations operating under conditions of explicit work rules related to seniority and other rights to jobs, promotion, pensions, and to the settlement of disputes. But this is not always the case. There is never complete insurance against job loss when demand declines, and large organizations are frequently an important employer of part-time labor (e.g., department stores).

Moreover, even in those organizations in which internal labor markets are well developed, potential promotional sequences are not available for all workers. In banking, for example, executives and professionals may enjoy opportunities for advancement, while office clericals may find their employment essentially a dead-end street.

It may even be argued that there are some offsetting advantages to workers employed in small or medium-sized firms. Small organizations are less bureaucratized, and the performance of the worker is more visible to his employer. If the worker is highly effective, he or she will tend to stand out and may be more readily rewarded on the basis of merit, presuming, of course, that there are positions of responsibility to which he or she can be promoted. In addition, the small enterprise requires little capital and is readily organized, so that individuals with sufficient skill and initiative may find rewards through opening up their own businesses in industries characterized by small size.

Regardless of these considerations, however, small-scale operations tend to have very flat hierarchical structures and, accordingly, offer limited opportunities for advancement, whatever may be the intelligence, dedication, and initiative of the individual worker. Perhaps as important, the record shows that the failure rate in such activities is high.

Table 3.8 presents evidence of job protection for each occupation-industry cell in the services (1970) in terms of three employment characteristics: percentage of workers with collective bargaining coverage (only 30 percent of more shown); percentage of workers licensed or accredited (only 30 percent or more shown); extent of internal labor market (only cells in which opportunities for advancement were well developed—"Considerable"—or moderately well developed—"Moderate"—are identified).*

In addition, two measures of establishment and firm size are given for each industry: median establishment size (in terms of number of employers) and extent of industrial concentration (classified within a five-way classification, ranging from "high" to "atomistic").†

The juxtaposition of the several measures in Table 3.8 is revealing. We observe that only in transportation, communication, utilities, FIRE, and public administration is there evidence of significant sheltering except for professionals (across all industries), technicians (in health services) and nonoffice clericals (several industries). Moreover, certain occupations appear to offer very little or no sheltering or opportunities for advancement through internal labor market "laddering," regardless of industry. This is the case for office clericals, sales workers, and service workers (outside the TCU industries)—the occupations which contain the largest proportion of "female-labeled" employment.

The measures pertaining to size are of special interest in indicating those industries in which firms and separate establishments operated by corporations are typically small and those industries in which they are large. The services are seen to vary sharply in terms of median establishment size and degree of concentration. The TCU industries are characterized by large median size and high levels of concentration, as is public administra-

---

*These measures were developed by Marcia Freedman for her analysis in *Labor Markets: Segment and Shelters* (1976) and were taken from her worksheets. Dr. Freedman's sources are presented in that volume on pp. 170–75. In defining the internal labor market classifications she states, "if a considerable number, but not all, of the subgroups in a given (industry-occupation) cell offer employed workers the possibility of vertical movement at a given market site, that cell is designated as 'moderate'. If the majority of the subgroups have internal pyramiding, the cell is designated as 'considerable.'" Data more recent than 1970 are not available.

†See footnote c in Table 3.8.

Table 3.8 Evidence of Sheltering and Internal Labor Markets in the U.S. Economy, 1970

	Professionals	Technicians	Managers	Office clericals	Nonoffice clericals	Sales workers	Craftsmen	Operatives	Service workers	Laborers	Industry Characteristics[a]	Extent of Industrial Concentration[b]
Trucking and Warehousing	100**				**50		**80	**80	**80	**80	51–300	Lo
Transportation	84***	61*55	*M57	**56	*M76		**90	**90	**90	**90	901+	Hi
Communications	79C*	*M55	C*	**40	*M80		*C80	**80	*M80	**80	901+	Hi
Utilities	89C*	*M*	*C*		*M40		*C80	*M80	*M80	*M80	901+	Hi
Wholesale	82**				*M*		**31	**39			21–50	At-Lo
Retail, nondurable	93**				*M*		**35	**30			21–50	At-Lo
Retail, durable	93**							*47			21–50	At-Lo
FIRE	84C*	59M*	*C*		*C*	99**	**37				301–900	Mo

Industry						Median establishment size[a]	Extent of industrial concentration[b]
Producer services	84**				35**	1-20	At
Health Services	79**	73**	*M*	*M*	35**	21-50	At-Lo
Education, Welfare	67 M**	41**			27**	901+	Hi
Restaurants, Hotels	83**		*M*	*M*		1-20	At
Personal, Repair services	65**	*30			30**	1-20	At
Public administration	62 C*	C49	*C*	C45	C76	M49 40** M40 40**	901+	Hi

a Median establishment size in number of workers.

b Extent of industrial concentration: *Hi* (High): output of top four firms represents over 50 percent or more of total output within its market and total number of sellers is not large. *Mo* (Moderate): output of top four firms is 35–50 percent of output and there are hundreds of sellers. *Lo* (Low): output of top four firms is less than 35 percent of output, with largest controlling about 6–8 percent. *At-Lo* (A combination type): has significant sectors of two types, one atomistic and one low or moderate. *At* (Atomistic): has many sellers, no one of which controls a significant part of the market.

Note: Code for sheltering measures in each cell: *Upper left:* Percentage of workers licensed or accredited (only percentages of 30 or more shown). *Middle:* Internal labor market (M equals moderate, C equals considerable. See footnote page 00). *Lower right:* Collective bargaining coverage (only percentages of 30 or more shown). Asterisk indicates measure is relatively unimportant. If none of sheltering measures is important, cell is left empty.

Source: Compiled from worksheets from Marcia Freedman, *Labor Markets: Segments and Shelters* (Montclair, N.J.: Allanheld, Osmun, 1976). See pages 170–75 of her book for further explanations and sources of data.

tion. FIRE employment falls in the middle range in terms of median establishment size, and the component industries are characterized by moderate concentration. The remaining service industry groups are largely small in scale with low levels of concentration.

When this evidence is related to what we have learned about the distribution of jobs by occupation and industry, the structure of earnings, and the availability of employment to females and to blacks, the picture is a highly consistent one. The services offer employment opportunities that are sharply divided in terms of prospects for good pay and advancement, with relatively few of the better positions available for women and minorities.

PART-TIME EMPLOYMENT

A major factor contributing to the low earnings levels of many workers in the services is the tendency to work less than fulltime. Table 3.9 provides solid evidence of this tendency. In the services, taken as a whole, the percentage of employment which was less than full time, full year in 1975 was 43.5, while in the nonservices, it was 37.1.

Yet there is considerable variation among services industries, as well as among occupations within industries. In the distributive services, public administration, and FIRE, part-time work accounts for less than 30 percent of total employment; in retailing and consumer services, the shares are 55 percent and 64 percent (Table 3.9). Taken as a whole, part-time work is found most frequently among service workers and laborers, and least frequently among professionals, managers, and technicians.

Conclusion

A major conclusion of this chapter is that changes observed in the structure of occupation and earnings of the U.S. workforce find their explanation largely in the shift of employment from goods-to service-producing activities, and to a more limited extent in the differential of growth between white and blue collar occupations in both the service and nonservice industries.

Occupation and earnings characteristics of employment in the

Table 3.9 Less than Full-Time, Full-Year Employment Share in Each Industry-Occupational Subgroup in the United States, 1975 (in percentages)

	Professionals	Technicians	Managers	Office clericals	Nonoffice clericals	Sales workers	Craftsmen	Operatives	Service workers	Laborers	All occupations
All industry (total US)	34.7	32.2	17.4	38.9	44.6	48.4	34.9	43.9	65.3	62.5	41.4
Construction	7.4	14.8	24.4	47.3	21.6	33.9	57.9	59.3	75.7	71.0	52.3
Manufacturing	13.1	15.0	10.4	27.0	27.4	54.6	26.1	42.0	37.3	46.4	31.9
Distributive services	12.4	25.5	11.4	35.0	26.2	17.8	14.8	39.3	55.8	45.2	26.3
TCU	11.6	27.3	11.2	25.7	22.3	23.1	13.0	39.2	50.2	42.9	25.9
Wholesale	14.2	15.2	11.5	42.0	36.4	17.6	21.7	39.6	78.8	49.3	26.8
Retail	27.0	50.4	21.3	47.1	66.7	62.3	31.0	56.9	74.6	70.4	54.6
Producer services	20.6	29.2	15.6	40.3	38.7	30.5	32.4	53.2	55.4	70.2	32.8
FIRE	17.4	15.4	15.2	35.2	31.2	30.1	32.3	38.5	45.0	73.1	28.3
Corporate services	21.5	36.8	16.4	48.3	61.6	35.7	32.5	54.8	61.6	66.0	38.8
Consumers services	41.3	72.1	23.1	59.5	68.8	74.6	35.3	53.9	76.9	87.8	63.9
Nonprofit services	47.2	47.5	23.3	45.9	66.2	45.2	27.5	40.5	55.4	59.4	48.4
Health	27.7	41.6	15.4	40.7	39.0	55.8	15.5	32.5	45.3	38.6	39.0
Education	48.4	63.6	29.4	49.8	74.9	42.2	36.8	51.2	69.7	67.5	54.4
Public administration	15.8	12.0	11.1	27.0	21.7	42.4	22.1	24.7	48.3	41.3	20.7
Services (total)	38.3	36.2	17.6	40.9	48.0	47.7	25.6	46.4	66.3	63.5	43.5
Nonservices (total)	13.1	16.4	17.0	30.8	26.8	54.2	41.4	42.7	39.8	61.8	37.1

Source: U.S. Bureau of the Census, *Survey of Income and Education*, 1976.

services industries vary considerably among themselves and when compared with the nonservice industries. Most of the distributive industries as well as the public sector tend to resemble closely the pattern that prevails in a number of nonservice industries. Earnings are relatively high, the share of medium-range jobs tends to be large, and there appears to be considerable internal laddering of the sort necessary to provide workers' promotion or, at least, to provide expectations of earnings upgrading. Most other service industries offer earning and occupational structures highly bifurcated between well-paid, relatively sheltered professionals, managers, and technicians, and poorly paid, relatively unsheltered clericals, laborers, and service workers. Among this second group of services, there are two different patterns, however. Producer (FIRE and corporate services) and nonprofit services (mostly health services) tend to employ large numbers of professionals, semiprofessionals, and technicians, and their low-skilled workers — despite an environment characterized by a general lack of opportunities for occupational and earnings upgrading — tend to enjoy earnings relatively higher than those of their counterparts in the remaining service industries — retailing and consumer services. These latter services not only offer mostly low-skilled occupations with blocked paths to advancement, but simultaneously tend to pay poorly. Although largely a reflection of heavy reliance on part-time employees, this characteristic is worrisome in light of the predominance of women and minority workers in these industries.

While not necessarily as important in terms of the overall magnitude of its impact on employment systems, the shift away from blue collar work is one that is being felt among many industries — especially among nonservice firms where technology is rapidly replacing traditional blue collar occupations and where servicelike functions (management, engineering, research, advertising, etc.) are proliferating.

A major observation of this chapter is that the combination of these two shifts — toward services and toward white collar work — is bringing about an increased bifurcation in both the structure of earnings distribution and the structure of job opportunities in the nation's labor force, with a growing separation between relatively good jobs and relatively bad jobs.

A final key observation is that while the recent transformation of the nation's labor market has been marked by a sharp increase in the participation of female (both white and minority) workers, females have entered mostly low-skilled and low-paid occupations and have shown, thus far, extremely limited success in improving their position. At the same time, data presented in this chapter suggest even greater reasons to worry about the future of black male workers, since they indicate that this group of workers is encountering serious difficulties in finding its place in a mostly white collar workforce.

In the next chapter, we attempt to determine the extent to which these findings are applicable in understanding the transformation of metropolitan labor markets.

CHAPTER 4

Learning about Metropolitan Labor Markets from the Continuous Work History Sample

The preceding analysis has disclosed much regarding the nature and significance of the growth of the service industries and the transformation from blue to white collar work for employment in the American economy as a whole. What has not been demonstrated is the extent to which generalizations regarding the special characteristics associated with individual industries are applicable to individual metropolitan labor markets. This chapter is an attempt to resolve this issue and to further specify the implications of such industry employment characteristics for individual labor markets.

The lack of appropriate detailed statistics has been a formidable obstacle to analysis of labor market conditions in specific places in the past. Only in years covered by the decennial census have limited data for sex, race, occupation, and industry been available. For intervening years, employment data for most metropolitan areas are available only on an industry basis, without sex and race breakdowns and with little or no information regarding earnings or other job attributes, such as extent of part-time work.*

The Social Security Continuous Work History Sample Materials

For more than a decade (1957–1975) a major source of labor market information has been in limited use in urban and regional research: the Continuous Work History Sample (CWHS) based on the national social security files. These data are unique in that they follow the individuals sampled through time, so that the data record not only the employment in a given area at a given date but also the flows of workers into and out of the covered work force. The sample of the CWHS data file provides, on a county basis (which can be combined for SMSAs, states and regions), annual information by sex and race and by two-digit SIC industry for the following groups of workers:†

1. *Stayers:* persons currently in the covered workforce who were in the same industry at the beginning of the period chosen.

2. *New entrants:* persons currently in the covered workforce who were not in the covered workforce anywhere at the beginning of the period.

3. *Inmigrants:* persons currently in the covered workforce who were in the covered work force at another location at the beginning of the period.

4. *Job in-movers:* persons currently in the covered workforce in a given industry who were in another covered industry but in the same location at the beginning of the period.

5. *Departures:* persons who were in the covered workforce at the beginning of the period but are no longer in the covered workforce (largely retirees).

6. *Outmigrants:* persons who were in the covered workforce at

---

*These sources are primarily the *County Business Patterns* of the Bureau of the Census of the Department of Commerce and the *Employment and Earnings* series of the Bureau of Labor Statistics of the Department of Labor.

†Social security reports are filed quarterly by employers, but the files made available to researchers are adjusted to an annual basis.

the beginning of the period who are in the covered workforce elsewhere at the end of the period.

7. *Job out-movers:* persons who were in the covered work force in a given industry at the beginning of the period who are in another covered industry in the same location at the end of the period.

The major limitations of these data are: (a) the small size of the samples: until recently only a 1-percent sample has been available, which renders much of the most interesting analysis of possible subgroups statistically unreliable except for very large SMSAs, states, or regions; and (b) the restriction of coverage to workers within the social security system: persons employed by government, including most public school teachers (but typically not universities and hospitals), are for the most part omitted, as are self-employed who, until recently, were not part of the system.*

Like the regularly published data sources, the CWHS material provides no occupational breakdown. It does, however, provide information relating to average earnings of the various worker groups by industry, subclassified by sex and race, as well as information regarding age of workers.

Recently the Department of Commerce has made available for research use CWHS materials based on a 10-percent sample for the period 1971 through 1975. The increase in sample size opens up important opportunities for a more careful analysis of urban labor markets than has up to now been possible. This new data base provides the major source of information for the analyses that follow in this chapter and in Chapter 6. Unfortunately, the form under which the data are currently made available limits the analysis in several ways. First, the industry classification system, which the Department of Commerce uses at the moment for its 10-percent sample, is more restricted than that used in the 1-percent sample or that presented in the previous chapters. As Table 4.1 shows, the data are classified under very broad groupings, which include in some instances relatively heterogeneous combinations. This is particularly troublesome in the case of the "other services" category, which lumps the intermediate corporate services with consumer services and nonprofit services, and in the

---

*In recent years most self-employed persons have been allowed and have elected to become a part of the Social Security system.

Table 4.1   Comparison of Classification Systems

10-percent sample of CWHS classification (Chapters 4 and 6)	Stanback and Noyelle classification (Chapters 2, 3, 5)
Construction	Construction
Manufacturing	Manufacturing
TCU (Transportation, Communication, and Utilities)	TCU
Wholesale/Retail	Wholesale Retail
FIRE (Finance, Insurance and Real estate)	FIRE
Other services	Corporate services Consumer services Nonprofit services
(not covered)	Government

Note: The 10-percent sample of the CWHS relies on 1-digit S.I.C. groupings. The classification scheme we use throughout Chapters 2, 3 and 5 consists of a grouping of 2-digit SIC industries. It is discussed in Chapter 2 and presented in detail in Appendix Table 1.

case of wholesale and retail services, which we have seen differ significantly in occupational structure and earnings distribution. Second, researchers are provided not with tapes but with printouts, in which only certain tabulations are presented in a standardized format.* It is these tabulations that provided the basis for the analysis presented hereafter.

The tabulations do not provide the information necessary to carry through true cohort analysis. One cannot select two or more groups of workers defined in some specific way (e.g., by age, sex, or race), follow them through time, and compare experiences in terms of, say, earnings levels attained or interindustry mobility. One can compare, however, for those periods for which the data are available, size and average earnings of various sex, race, and

*Many of the current restrictions on the use of the 10-percent sample have to do with the issue of public disclosure.

age subgroups within the industry categories provided. More important, the number and average earnings of each of the seven groups of workers described above (e.g., stayers, new entrants, etc.) are provided for the industry groups and are available by sex, race, and age.

The total span of years (1971–1975) for which these new data are available has been conveniently broken down by the Department of Commerce into two periods, 1971–73 and 1973–75. 1973 being a peak year and 1975 a recession year, the first span of years enables us to examine employment flows during a period of expansion; the second, during a period of contraction.

To summarize, the 10-percent sample provides valuable research material in a form suitable for SMSA analysis. At the same time, it is significantly more restricted in terms of the range and level of detail of information available to the researcher than is the 1-percent sample.

Are National Employment Characteristics of Industries Applicable at the SMSA Level?

A major finding stated in the previous chapter was that very significant differences in occupation, sex composition, and earnings levels could be observed among industries. It is of critical importance to learn whether or not industry employment characteristics have broad generality or simply represent an averaging for the nation of dissimilar characteristics in the various SMSAs and other urban and rural places that make up the national employment system.

Indeed, it is implicit in our earlier (Chapter 2) analysis of industrial composition of SMSAs that employment in given industries, wherever found, represents roughly similar work being performed and similar occupational composition. If such were not true, at least to a significant degree, this traditional and widely used approach to urban and regional analysis would be of little value.

It should be stressed, however, that there is no reason to expect occupational structure, earnings, and other characteristics of given industrial groupings to be identical in different

Table 4.2   Female Employment Share and Relative Levels of Annual Earnings (both sexes) by Industry Groups: United States and Average of Seven SMSAs, 1975

	Female employment (%)			Annual earnings[a] (both sexes)		
	U.S. average	7 SMSAs		U.S. average	7 SMSAs	
		Averages[b]	Range[c]		Average[b]	Range[c]
All industries	39.7	40.7	39.2–42.8	1.00	1.00	not applicable
Construction	5.2	8.8	5.8–10.4	1.09	1.16	1.03–1.27
Manufacturing	29.6	25.8	20.3–40.4	1.16	1.16	0.89–1.23
TCU	21.6	25.7	19.8–29.9	1.37	1.40	1.27–1.53
Wholesale/Retail	44.5	42.4	39.1–49.8	0.76	0.82	0.66–0.96
FIRE	52.2	54.4	47.4–58.8	1.12	1.08	0.97–1.17
Other services	59.0	60.3	55.5–63.7	0.89	0.89	0.83–0.99

[a] Annual earnings have been converted to indexes (average earnings for U.S. and for each SMSA equal 1.0) to adjust for differences in local and regional general wage levels. Average earnings for U.S. was $8,610. Modified average of average earnings in 7 places was $8,462.
[b] Modified averages. Highest and lowest values have been dropped.
[c] Highest and lowest values.

Source: U.S. Bureau of the Census, *Survey of Income and Education*, 1976, and U.S. Bureau of Economic Analysis, *Ten Percent Continuous Work History Sample*, 1971, 1973 and 1975.

metropolitan economies. Not only are such groupings rather broad, including dissimilar mixes of specific industry subgroups, but metropolitan economies (as we have seen) may be expected to vary in terms of the way manufacturing and service functions are carried out, depending upon size of the metropolitan economy and level of specialization of the activities concerned. Accordingly, it is useful at the outset to compare, between the United States and the seven selected SMSAs for each of the major industry groupings, two of these key employment characteristics: *percent female employment* and *average annual earnings* (both sexes).*
The earnings comparison is made in terms of relative earnings in-

*A rough comparison of occupational structures is not possible since such data are not available for the seven places from the CWHS material.

dexes in order to adjust for area differentials in dollar wage levels.*

In both sets of comparisons, the average values for the selected SMSAs (Table 4.2) in given industries are found to be similar to the comparable national statistics. We observe that there are variations among places within industries, but such variations are generally smaller than variations among the industrial groupings themselves.

The greatest and most relevant industry variations (given the relative importance of the sector) are found in manufacturing, where percent female employment varies widely from 20 percent to 40 percent. This reflects differences among manufacturing industries that rely strongly on a female labor force (as with textiles in Charlotte) and others that traditionally have remained closed to women (as with automobiles or chemicals in Buffalo) (see next chapter).

Although these comparisons constitute an extremely simple analysis, they go far to support the hypothesis that there are important place-to-place similarities in employment characteristics of given industrial groupings. Each of the variables examined is highly significant for urban labor market analysis: the level of female employment, as we have seen, tends to be highly occupation specific; and the level of average earnings provides the single most important summary statistic of employment conditions.

But we do not have to rest the case that a number of employment characteristics are significantly industry-specific on the above comparisons. In the sections that follow additional analyses will point to similarity in composition of employment and in job characteristics among given industry groupings in different places.

Industrial Composition and Changes in Employment

DISTRIBUTION OF EMPLOYMENT AMONG INDUSTRIES

A fundamental observation of Chapter 2 is that metropolitan economies vary in terms of their industrial distributions of

---

*Annual earnings in each industry group have been converted to indexes in which average earnings for United States and for each SMSA are equivalent to 1.0.

employment. This is clearly evidenced in Table 4.3, which shows the seven SMSAs' average distribution of the covered workforce among industry groups, along with the highest and lowest SMSA shares for each industry. The range is greatest for manufacturing, indicating that one of the most important differences in industrial structure among places typically stems from variations in the relative importance of manufacturing and in types of manufactures. Shares of employment in wholesale/retail vary least in relative terms, reflecting the essentially local population-serving nature of its principal component, retailing. We know that, in fact, the wholesale sector does vary to a considerable degree in importance and that large wholesale and TCU sectors are characteristics of places acting as strong regional distribution centers. As regards construction, its importance is strongly influenced by the growth rate of the metropolitan economy. Finally, the variations in the size of the other services sector, which are quite large, can be associated with the strength of either their nonprofit sector, the business services, or the consumer services, depending on the place (see Chapter 5).

DISTRIBUTION OF MALE AND
FEMALE EMPLOYMENT BY INDUSTRY

Not unexpectedly, the industrial distribution of employment differs between male and female workers (Table 4.3). The average share of females who find employment in construction, manufacturing, and TCU is much lower than the average share of males. The shares of females and males in wholesale–retail are roughly the same, however, and the average shares of females in FIRE and other services are significantly higher—more than twice as high in the latter. These tendencies reflect the importance of female employment in industries with a large number of clerical and service-worker jobs.

INDUSTRIAL DISTRIBUTION OF
EMPLOYMENT AMONG BLACKS

Although industrial composition differs from place to place and the relative importance of blacks in the work force ranges widely, it is quite clear that blacks find employment more readily in some

Table 4.3 Average Distribution of Covered Workforce among Industry Groups by Sex and Race, in Seven SMSAs, 1973, (in percentages)

| | Entire covered workforce | | Males | | | | Females | | | |
| | All sex-race | | All races | | Blacks only | | All races | | Blacks only | |
	Average[a]	Range[b]	Average[a]	Range[b]	Average[a]	Range[b]	Average[a]	Range[b]	Average[a]	Range[b]
Construction	8.0	4.7–10.8	12.3	6.9–16.2	11.6	4.6–14.8	1.4	2.0–2.3	1.0	0.5–2.9
Manufacturing	27.1	15.5–35.6	30.1	19.0–46.3	33.3	25.5–59.8	19.4	9.9–34.0	20.9	12.5–37.5
TCU	6.7	4.9–10.0	8.2	6.3–13.4	7.2	4.0–11.1	4.2	3.0–5.8	4.5	2.0–8.6
Wholesale/Retail	27.9	23.4–31.7	27.6	20.1–30.6	23.7	11.5–28.7	28.9	25.7–33.4	19.5	14.3–25.0
FIRE	7.5	4.8–9.8	6.2	3.3–7.6	4.3	2.9–6.9	9.7	6.7–13.3	7.4	3.6–9.4
Other services	23.0	17.7–30.9	15.3	11.4–20.8	18.5	13.3–23.2	35.0	27.1–45.4	45.8	35.2–54.2

aModified averages. Highest and lowest rates have been dropped. Because these are modified averages, columns do not sum up exactly to 100 percent.
bHighest and lowest value of the range.

Source: U.S. Bureau of Economic Analysis, Ten Percent Continuous Work History Sample.

industries than others (Table 4.3).* Black males tend to be over-represented in manufacturing and other services as compared to all males, relatively underrepresented in the remaining industrial groups. Black females are slightly overrepresented in the important manufacturing category as compared to all females, heavily overrepresented in other services (on average, almost half of their total employment) — presumably largely as service workers. They are significantly underrepresented in wholesale-retail and FIRE. Although occupational data are not available, the finding that both black males and black females are hired much more frequently in those industries where blue collar and service worker jobs are most important indicates that they have been largely unsuccessful in finding employment in white collar jobs.†

GAINS AND LOSSES IN OVERALL SHARES OF EMPLOYMENT BY SEX-RACE GROUPS

Table 4.4 makes clear the extent of gains and losses in shares of total employment accounted for by white and black men and women and by other minorities. Shares of employment are shown for each sex-race group in each SMSA for 1975, along with changes in shares during the period covered (1971–1975). The general finding is that shares of the workforce accounted for by males, both blacks and whites, declined from 1971 to 1975 with the shift from goods to service employment, while shares accounted for by black and white females increased (with the single exception of Charlotte, where white males gained in importance).

Employment of the remaining minority group, "other," was not analyzed separately for males and females because of inadequate sample size. We observe that the group (males and females combined) increased in importance everywhere between 1971 and 1975, although 1975 shares were very small except in Denver and Phoenix.

---

*The CWHS files contain information on other minorities (grouped as "other"), but the relatively small number of these workers prohibits analysis of industrial distribution.

†Table 4.3 does not make clear the extent of the difference in percentages of black workers in the southern SMSAs on one hand and the remaining SMSAs on the other. Nashville, Atlanta, and Charlotte show shares of male and female covered workers accounted for by blacks of 7 to 11 percent. In the remaining SMSAs percentages range from 1.3 to 4.9.

Table 4.4 Distribution of Covered Workforce by Sex and Race, 1975; Change in Distribution (shares) 1971–1975, Seven SMSAs; Tallies of Gains and Losses by Sex and Race during the 1971–1973 and 1973–1975 Periods

| | Shares of covered workforce (%), 1975 | | | | | Changes in shares (%) = 1971–1975 | | | | |
| | Male | | Female | | | Male | | Female | | |
	White	Black	White	Black	Other[a]	White	Black	White	Black	Other[a]
Atlanta	48.3	10.9	31.4	8.9	0.5	-4.7	-0.1	3.0	1.8	NC
Denver	55.7	2.1	38.1	1.7	2.4	-3.3	-0.1	2.8	0.1	0.5
Buffalo	56.6	3.8	36.0	3.0	0.7	-1.3	-0.5	1.6	0.2	0.1
Phoenix	54.3	1.5	39.2	1.3	3.7	-3.2	-0.2	2.6	0.1	0.7
Columbus	53.9	4.9	36.6	4.0	0.5	-3.3	-0.5	3.0	0.5	0.2
Nashville	49.6	7.4	35.9	6.8	0.3	-1.9	-0.6	1.9	0.4	0.2
Charlotte	50.0	10.1	31.9	7.4	0.5	0.6	-0.7	-0.9	0.8	0.1
Tally: Number of SMSAs	1971–1973					1973–1975				
Gains	–	3	5	5	*	1	–	7	5	*
Losses	6	2	2	1	*	6	7	–	1	*
No change	1	2	–	2	*	0	–	–	1	*

a "Other": other minority, male and female combined.
*Not shown because of small sample size.

Source: U.S. Bureau of Economic Analysis, Ten Percent Continuous Work History Sample.

The tallies of gains and losses in shares for the various groups in the seven SMSAs during subperiods 1971–1973 and 1973–1975 provide an indication of the effect of general economic expansion and contraction on tendencies of the several groups to gain or lose relative position. White males tended to lose during both periods; black males gained or held their shares of employment in five out of seven SMSAs during the expansion years, but lost ground everywhere between 1973 and the recession year 1975. Both white and black females showed gains in most places during both periods.

Earnings by Industry, by Sex and Race, and by Groups of Workers

One of the most attractive features of the CWHS materials is that they permit the researcher to separate stayers, those workers who are most permanently attached to the workforce in each industry, from those who have recently entered the SMSA workforce as new entrants or inmigrants, or who have transferred from one industry to another.* In this section we examine for each industry the average earnings levels of male and female workers in each of these groups (i.e. stayers, new entrants, inmigrants, and job movers). Here the analysis focuses on white workers, since sample size of minorities in these subsets is too small for statistical reliability.

A SECOND LOOK AT THE NATIONAL DATA

Before presenting these analyses, it is important to recall that the CWHS data are not available by occupation or in a form that permits a distribution of employment by earnings brackets. Information regarding earnings is available only in the form of an average

---

*It was not until this monograph was in galley form that the authors read the excellent study by Barry Bluestone, Patricia Hanna, Sarah Kuhn, and Laura Moore, *The Retail Revolution* (Boston: Auburn House Publishing Co., 1981). This study makes use of the 1-percent Social Security Continuous Work History Sample LEED Files to examine wages and mobility characteristics of workers in retailing in New England. Bluestone et al.'s findings agree with and, to a considerable extent, amplify ours reported in this and the following chapters.

for each group of workers (stayers, new entrants, etc.) within each industrial classification.

Accordingly, it is useful to look once again at the earnings distribution of employment by industry group as derived in Chapter 3 for the nation for such insights as these data afford.* Since two of the industrial groupings (wholesale/retail and other services) utilized in the CWHS materials are different from those presented in Chapter 3, the distributions have been recomputed in Table 4.5 to match the CWHS groupings.

Summary statements regarding the various industries may be made as follows:

1. *Construction* is heavily weighted in the middle-income brackets and is characterized by an extremely low proportion of female employees (5 percent). This distribution is strongly influenced by well-paid and usually unionized craftsmen (Table 3.1).

2. *Manufacturing* is strongly weighted in the middle and upper income brackets with little employment in the lower brackets. Here we see the influence of unions and internal labor markets, which guarantee that a sizeable number of employees will move up the income ladders over the years of their tenure. For the industry as a whole, women represent close to 30 percent of the labor force.

3. *TCU* is relatively heavily weighted in the middle and upper income brackets with virtually no employment in the lower brackets. This distribution is strongly influenced by craftsmen and operatives (Table 3.1) (largely men with well-paid jobs). For the industry group as a whole the percentage of female employment is small, 22 percent.

4. The combined *wholesale-retail* industry group reflects principally the earnings distribution of the largest component, retailing. Female employment is relatively high (44 percent) and the low paying occupations, non-office clericals (which include retail sales checkout clerks), sales workers, and service workers, account for 50 percent of all jobs (Table 3.1). Almost half of all workers in wholesale-retail employment is found in industry-occupation cells in which average earnings are less than 80 percent of the national average.

*The earnings distributions are based on the 1975 *Survey of Income and Education.*

Table 4.5 Distribution of Employment among Earnings Classes by Industry and for Total United States, 1975 (in percentages)

	1.60 and above	1.20 to 1.59	0.80 to 1.19	0.40 to 0.79	0.39 and below	Share of females (percentage)
All industry (total U.S.)	12.0	22.2	27.8	28.4	9.6	39.7
Construction	2.5	17.2	61.1	18.3	0.3	5.2
Manufacturing	20.4	17.4	45.0	17.2	–	29.6
TCU	20.9	41.0	36.1	2.0	–	21.6
Wholesale/Retail	12.2	7.5	30.1	47.8	2.4	44.5
Wholesale	48.5	8.8	21.9	10.8	1.0	23.9
Retail	–	7.1	32.9	57.1	2.9	49.3
FIRE	18.5	32.7	2.3	46.5	–	52.2
Other services	6.6	23.0	10.9	37.0	22.5	59.0

Note: Earnings class intervals make use of earnings indexes in which 1.0 is equal to the U.S. average earnings per worker in 1975 ($8,610). For an explanation of the method used to distribute employment by earnings class, see Chapter 3.

Source: U.S. Bureau of the Census, *Survey of Income and Education*, 1976.

5. *FIRE* is essentially bimodal, with more than 50 percent of the employees earning 120 percent or more of the national average (professionals, technicians, and sales workers — largely men — see Table 3.1), and more than 46 percent earning less than 80 percent (largely female clerical workers — see Table 3.6).

6. The heterogeneous *other services* category, which is a combination of the predominantly low-income consumer services and of the more bimodally distributed producer and nonprofit services (Table 3.3), is, itself, somewhat bimodally distributed: 60 percent of workers in subgroups with earnings less than 80 percent of the national average; 10 percent in the 80–119 percent range; 23 percent between 120 and 159 percent of the national average; and almost 7 percent in the 160 percent and more bracket. Occupationally the group is heavily overrepresented at the top by professionals (27 percent) and at the bottom by service workers (27 percent) (Table 3.1). Almost 60 percent of employment is female (Table 3.6).

With these findings in mind, we can now return to a presentation of the CWHS data.

EARNINGS OF STAYERS

Table 4.6 shows the average distribution of employment and the average earnings level by industry for both white male and white female stayers. In the case of the wholesale-retail industry grouping, it was possible to estimate a rough disaggregation of the two sectors (see Appendix 2).*

The general findings for white male stayers are that average earnings of this relatively stable and mature group of workers are highest in the distributive services (TCU and wholesale) and in FIRE and other services (the latter being a combination of the dissimilar producer and consumer services); earnings are lowest in retail. Averages for construction and manufacturing fall between these two extremes and are just under 1.50 percent of the average overall SMSA earnings.

These observations need to be interpreted in the light of what we have learned from the national data regarding industrial

---

*Ideally we should have done the same for the other service sector, but its highly composite nature made such estimation quite unreliable.

Table 4.6 Average Distribution of Covered Workforce and Average Earning Levels by Industry among White Male and White Female Stayers; Ratio of Earnings of White Female to White Male Stayers by Industry, Seven SMSAs, 1973

| | White male stayers | | | White female stayers | | | Ratio of earnings | |
| | Employment distribution | Earnings[b] | | Employment distribution | Earnings[b] | | White female stayers to white male stayers | |
	Average[a]	Average[c]	Range[d]	Average[a]	Average[c]	Range[d]	Average	Range
All industry	100.0	1.56	1.44–1.63	100.0	0.81	0.74–0.88	0.52	0.50–0.57
Construction	9.2	1.49	1.38–1.55	1.2	0.95	0.73–1.13	0.65	0.56–0.77
Manufacturing	37.5	1.47	1.26–1.61	22.5	0.81	0.57–0.92	0.55	0.45–0.60
TCU	9.9	1.79	1.55–2.01	5.2	1.18	0.93–1.22	0.64	0.60–0.70
Wholesale/Retail	23.6	1.44	1.26–1.61	25.0	0.63	0.46–0.72	0.44	0.37–0.48
Wholesale[e]	(9.4)	(1.70)		(4.3)	(0.83)			
Retail[e]	(14.2)	(1.24)		(20.7)	(0.59)			
FIRE	5.6	1.95	1.56–1.99	9.3	0.88	0.76–0.96	0.46	0.44–0.49
Other services	12.9	1.75	1.55–1.81	35.1	0.86	0.76–0.95	0.50	0.43–0.55

[a]These are modified averages of shares (%) of covered employment for the seven places. Accordingly the columns do not sum exactly to 100.0 for all industries.

[b]For a definition of earning indexes see footnote [a], Table 4.2. Average earning level of all covered workforce equals 1.0 for each SMSA.

[c]Modified averages. Highest and lowest values have been dropped.

[d]Highest and lowest values.

[e]Estimates – see text and appendix 2.

Source: U.S. Bureau of Economic Analysis, *Ten Percent Continuous Work History Sample.*

distribution of earnings. TCU and wholesale pay relatively well across occupations (Table 3.2) and show favorable earnings distributions (Table 4.5). Apparently white male stayers have achieved rather high earnings largely because these industries pay relatively well across the range of occupations. Manufacturing and construction show somewhat lower-level earnings, but the situation may be regarded as relatively favorable, since the data indicate that large numbers of workers have managed to move up to medium-earnings jobs. In FIRE and other services, where the distribution of earnings is bifurcated, we seem to be observing a more narrow group of male stayers made up mostly of well-paid professionals and managers (see Table 3.2). Finally, the data for retailing point to a situation in which workers who remain in the industry enjoy few prospects for advancement or favorable earnings. This observation is consistent with the earlier findings based on Table 3.2, which showed that all occupations in retailing ranked at or near the bottom of the earnings scale.

The most striking finding regarding white female stayers is that, except in the TCU industries, their average earnings fail consistently to reach the covered work force average for the SMSA (1.00)! Not surprisingly, the worst record is in the retail sector, which also happens to employ the second-largest group of white female stayers.

The ratios of female earnings to male earnings (Table 4.6) deserve careful attention. By and large they are highly consistent from place to place in each industry group but vary significantly across industry lines. Among the service industries only the TCU ratio, .64, is as high or higher than that for manufacturing. The remaining service industries are sharply lower: .50 for other services, .46 for FIRE, and .44 for wholesale-retail. To recall, these latter include close to 70 percent of the jobs in which the white female stayers are to be found.

Thus, a major finding is that even among stayers women's jobs in the services are likely to remain very poorly paid. The levels of the ratios, 50 percent or less (except for TCU), are particularly surprising in view of the fact that women's wages are generally considered to average roughly 60 percent of the men's. We can only conclude that the lower average earnings levels reflect substantial part-time employment.

Table 4.7   Average Earning Levels of Stayers and New Entrants, White Males and White Females, Seven SMSAs, 1973

	Stayers	New entrants	Ratio of Earnings: New entrants
	Average[a]	Average[a]	to stayers
White males			
All industry	1.56	0.67	0.43
Construction	1.49	0.75	0.50
Manufacturing	1.47	0.82	0.56
TCU	1.79	0.77	0.43
Wholesale/Retail	1.44	0.50	0.35
FIRE	1.95	0.92	0.47
Other services	1.75	0.75	0.43
White females			
All industry	0.81	0.41	0.51
Construction	0.95	0.44	0.46
Manufacturing	0.81	0.51	0.63
TCU	1.18	0.64	0.54
Wholesale/Retail	0.63	0.31	0.49
FIRE	0.88	0.55	0.62
Other services	0.86	0.46	0.53

[a]Modified average of indexes for seven places. Highest and lowest values dropped. Range is not shown. See Table 4.2.

Source: U.S. Bureau of Economic Analysis, *Ten Percent Continuous Work History Sample.*

EARNINGS OF NEW ENTRANTS

Table 4.7 shows the 1973 average earning levels of white male and white female groups of stayers and new entrants. The earnings achievement of the stayers can be looked upon as a rough indication of what lies in store for those workers who have recently entered the workforce.

The ratio of earnings of new entrants to stayers indicates that, among new entrants, women enter at earnings levels that are closer to the earnings levels of stayers for given industries than in the case for white males. This clearly indicates that women typically face stricter limitations on levels of earnings they can hope to achieve during their working lives (i.e., as stayers). The overwhelming characteristic of work for women is that their earnings expectations remain quite dismal: at best, they can hope to move from *very bad* earning levels as new entrants (about 40 percent of the overall SMSA average) to *poor* earning levels as stayers (about 80 percent of the overall SMSA average).

For men the future looks more promising, although, as we saw earlier, achievements in the retail sector (and possibly by extension in the consumer service sector) may not be as high as the combined wholesale-retail figures make it appear. One interesting finding is that the level of earnings for white male new entrants in FIRE is quite high (92 percent of the overall SMSA average). It seems probable that white male new entrants in FIRE are mostly persons entering as junior professionals and paraprofessionals, presumably after having gone through a period of college education.

In general however, the service industries offer beginning workers, both male and female, lower earnings relative to stayers than do manufacturing. Long-term earning achievements appear extremely restricted for females in almost all industries, and much better for males, at least in most sectors. This indicates that on the whole females (and most likely all other minority workers) typically suffer from being stuck in bad jobs. These conclusions should be tempered, however, by the observation that the difference between the earnings of new entrants and stayers is accounted for in part by a greater importance of part-time work among new entrants. Moreover, this is generally a more important consideration in retailing and in consumer services (part of other services) than in the other industrial groupings.

EARNINGS OF INMIGRANTS AND JOB MOVERS

Table 4.8 presents some indications of the earning profiles of inmigrants and job movers as compared to stayers and new entrants. Two observations are worth stating. (1) Typically, job movers receive lower earnings than inmigrants but, of course, higher earnings than new entrants. This is true for both men and women in service industries and in manufacturing. (2) In-

Table 4.8 Ratios of Earnings of New Entrants, Job Movers, and Immigrants to Earnings of Stayers, White Males and White Females, Average for Seven SMSAs, 1973

White Males

	Ratios: New entrants to stayers		Ratios: Job movers to stayers		Ratios: Immigrants to stayers	
	Average[a]	Range	Average[a]	Range	Average[a]	Range
All industries	0.43	0.41–0.48	0.66	0.62–0.71	0.80	0.72–0.92
Construction	0.50	0.46–0.55	0.73	0.67–0.88	0.80	0.73–0.84
Manufacturing	0.56	0.50–0.64	0.76	0.71–0.92	0.94	0.76–1.13
TCU	0.43	0.41–0.53	0.57	0.49–0.58	0.76	0.68–0.87
Wholesale/Retail	0.35	0.30–0.38	0.65	0.59–0.65	0.80	0.72–0.90
FIRE	0.47	0.42–0.50	0.62	0.49–0.72	0.73	0.67–1.03
Other services	0.43	0.39–0.50	0.54	0.47–0.59	0.67	0.59–0.77

White females

	Ratios: New entrants to stayers		Ratios: Job movers to stayers		Ratios: Immigrants to stayers	
	Average[a]	Range	Average[a]	Range	Average[a]	Range
All industries	0.51	0.48–0.56	0.76	0.73–0.84	0.79	0.67–0.86
Construction	0.46	0.38–0.54	0.78	0.64–0.87	0.68	0.49–0.82
Manufacturing	0.63	0.54–0.72	0.84	0.71–1.18	0.87	0.71–1.04
TCU	0.54	0.34–0.67	0.65	0.60–0.69	0.77	0.68–0.83
Wholesale/Retail	0.49	0.45–0.52	0.81	0.77–0.87	0.83	0.72–0.91
FIRE	0.62	0.58–0.65	0.75	0.70–0.84	0.78	0.73–0.88
Other services	0.53	0.46–0.60	0.66	0.57–0.73	0.78	0.67–0.84

[a]Modified average; highest and lowest values have been dropped.

Source: U.S. Bureau of Economic Analysis, *Ten Percent Continuous Work History Sample.*

migrants in the services tend to earn less relative to stayers in their industries than do inmigrants in manufacturing. A possible explanation is that, on average, manufacturing workers are more likely to possess skills that are industry-specific and, accordingly, are able to relocate in a firm within their industry on relatively favorable terms. The implication here is that, in general, migration on favorable earnings terms is more difficult in the services than in goods production.

Changes in Earnings

In this section we examine gains and losses in earning levels of all black males, white females, and black females relative to those of all white males. We then present estimates of the combined effect of the changes in employment composition on overall average earnings in each place.

CHANGES IN RELATIVE EARNINGS: BLACK MALES,
WHITE FEMALES, AND BLACK FEMALES COMPARED TO
WHITE MALES

Table 4.9 relates average earnings of white females, black males, and black females to those of white males and shows tendencies toward gains or losses during the two consecutive periods, 1971–73 and 1973–75.* Two general conclusions may be drawn from the data: first, that earnings of these groups are relatively low across industry lines and, second, that there was little or no improvement in relative earnings in most industdies over the entire 1971–75period. Only in TCU, where there is little female and minority employment, were there substantial gains.

The measures for total earnings (all industries) show that black males made gains in six SMSAs during the expansion period but lost or held their own in five places during the final period ending in the recession year 1975. On an industry-by-industry basis, they gained for the entire period relative to white males in manufacturing, TCU, and FIRE, but lost in the wholesale-retail and other

---

*Construction is not analyzed here since this industry employs very few women or minorities.

Table 4.9 Ratios of Earnings of Black Males, White Females, and Black Females to Earnings of White Males; Average for Seven SMSAs, 1971, 1973, and 1975; Tallies of Gains and Losses, 1971–1973 and 1973–1975

| | Earnings ratios[a] | | | Number of SMSAs with gains (losses) in earnings ratios | | | | | |
| | | | | 1971–73 | | | 1973–75 | | |
	1971	1973	1975	+	–	NC	+	–	NC
All industry									
BM	.64	.66	.65	6	–	1	2	4	1
WF	.52	.50	.50	–	7	–	4	–	3
BF	.45	.45	.48	3	2	2	7	0	0
Manufacturing									
BM	.68	.71	.71	5	1	1	4	3	–
WF	.53	.53	.52	1	5	1	4	3	–
BF	.47	.49	.48	5	2	–	3	3	1
TCU									
BM	.68	.70	.71	7	–	–	4	3	–
WF	.56	.59	.64	6	1	–	7	–	–
BF	.41	.52	.60	7	–	–	6	1	–
Wholesale/Retail									
BM	.64	.62	.62	3	4	–	4	3	–
WF	.45	.43	.43	–	7	–	4	1	2
BF	.38	.37	.40	3	4	–	5	1	1
FIRE									
BM	.51	.52	.53	4	3	–	4	3	–
WF	.48	.48	.48	1	3	3	3	–	3
BF	.37	.37	.40	2	2	3	7	–	–
Other services									
BM	.55	.52	.50	2	4	1	–	6	1
WF	.58	.55	.53	7	–	–	1	6	–
BF	.46	.46	.47	6	1	–	5	1	–

[a]Modified averages. Lowest and highest values have been dropped.

Key: + = gains; – = losses; NC = no change; BM = black males; WF = white females; and BF = black females.

Source: U.S. Bureau of Economic Analysis, *Ten Percent Continuous Work History Sample.*

services. Their relative earnings levels were particularly un-favorable in FIRE and other services, confirming the strong tendency toward stratification of employment in these segments of the labor market, which was noted in Chapter 3.

The failure of white females to gain in relative earnings in four of the five industry groups is surprising in light of their strong gains in employment. Relative earnings for all white females stood at only 50 percent of white males at the close of the period, and was no more than 53 percent of any industry group except TCU.

Black females fared best in terms of improving relative earnings but stood at the bottom of the hierarchy in earnings levels. Although they failed to make significant gains during the expansion period, their position improved in most industries in most places during the final years. Nevertheless, average earnings stood at only 48 percent of those of white males as the period close.

IMPACT OF CHANGING EMPLOYMENT COMPOSITION ON
AVERAGE SMSA EARNINGS

The overall result of substantial gains in shares of employment among poorly paid white and black females and losses in shares of employment among white males (with black males essentially holding their own) has resulted, not surprisingly, in a marked tendency for average per-worker earnings to decline in SMSAs.

This is shown in Table 4.10, which indicates the effect of increases in female and minority employment associated with the rise of services but does not reflect changes in relative earnings. Average per-worker earnings for 1971 are as shown in the CWHS materials. Average earnings for 1973 and 1975 have been adjusted to 1971 levels by holding earnings constant in each sex-race-industry subgroup, thereby measuring only the effect of changes in composition (sex, race, and industry) of the workforce. The resulting estimates show declines in average earnings in every SMSA except Charlotte during both periods.

The estimates do not make allowance for changes in overall wage levels or for the effects of inflation. We adjusted separately the 1973 and 1975 average per-worker earnings for each place in the CWHS materials by regional consumer price indexes to try to determine if the "real" earnings performance was superior to that shown in the adjusted estimates in Table 4.10. In every SMSA, deflated average earnings were found to have declined by greater amounts than the estimates that made use of 1971 average earnings. We concluded that inflation and other factors had contributed to make matters worse in terms of per-worker "real" earnings, and that for purposes of exposition of the effects of changing composition the estimates in Table 4.9 were the most appropriate.

It is important to put this finding in perspective. What we are observing is a tendency for declines to occur in average earnings per worker, yet, in light of increases in the number of workers per household, not necessarily in average earnings per capita.

Employment Opportunities

Traditionally, the two indexes that have most commonly been assumed to reflect labor market conditions are the rate of unemployment and the level of earnings. But there are other characteristics that relate to how well the job market functions, characteristics which concern the quality of jobs held.

To begin to understand the qualitative aspects of metropolitan labor markets, it is helpful to identify those industries in which there is high job turnover and those in which there is considerable stability. It is also important to assess the availability of employment (and the quality of that employment) for young people seeking their first jobs, as well as the opportunities for these workers to improve earnings and working conditions through promotions within the firm or through changing to better jobs in other firms and industries as they become more mature and experienced.

EMPLOYMENT TURNOVER

A basic and straightforward measure of employment turnover is found in the statistic, percentage of stayers, i.e., the percentage of persons in an industry workforce at the end of the period who were similarly employed at the beginning of the period. The significance of the measure lies in the fact that it reflects preferences of workers for remaining in a given industry, rather

Table 4.10 Effect of Sex-Race-Industry Shifts in the Labor Force on Average Earnings, 1971, 1973, and 1975, in Seven SMSAs

	Average earnings (in dollars)			Change (in dollars)	
	1971	1973	1975	1971–1973	1971–1975
Atlanta	7,511	7,325	7,139	−186	−372
Denver	7,206	7,134	7,031	−72	−175
Buffalo	7,192	7,131	7,133	−61	−59
Phoenix	6,444	6,422	6,272	−22	−172
Columbus	6,878	6,796	6,631	−82	−247
Nashville	6,113	6,079	6,059	−34	−54
Charlotte	6,444	6,448	6,469	+4	+25

Note: Average earnings for 1971 are as shown in the CWHS materials; average earnings for 1973 and 1975 were computed by applying the 1971 average earning in each sex-race industry subcategory to the 1973 and 1975 employment in the corresponding subcategory.

Source: U.S. Bureau of Economic Analysis, *Ten Percent Continuous Work History Sample.*

than moving about in search of better employment, as well as the ability of employers to offer such stable employment.

In an industry in which firms tend to promote from within and to provide considerable job security, the percentage of stayers may be expected to be higher than in an industry in which they do not. Similarly, in an industry in which there is considerable sheltering through well-recognized licensing or certification or through the influence of unions with resulting favorable wage structures, the percentage of stayers may also be expected to be relatively high.

Table 4.11 indicates distinct differences in average percentages of stayers among most industries. For males, TCU, which includes public utilities and telephone companies as well as the air and rail carriers (all typically large firms with strong sheltering), shows by far the highest average percentage of stayers (68 percent). Manufacturing ranks second (59 percent), presumably because of the protective influence of labor unions (or in some industries, such as textiles, the strong and continuing threat of labor union organization). The lowest shares of stayers tend to be found in wholesale-retail (predominantly retailing) and construction. For wholesale-retail the small average percentage of stayers (52 percent) is consistent with the earlier observation that retail wages are relatively low and that there is an almost complete absence of sheltering. Construction (50 percent), although well organized by labor unions in many places, offers relatively unstable work because of its strongly seasonal and cyclical pattern of employment. The intermediate positions of FIRE (55 percent) and other services (53 percent) would appear to reflect the heterogeneous nature of their composition. FIRE includes large banking and insurance firms but also small banks, insurance, and real estate offices. The large, catch-all "other services" category includes a variety of producer, consumer, and nonprofit services ranging from major hospitals and universities to legal offices, small producer, and consumer service firms. Moreover, there is a wide range of occupations including, on one hand, a number of professions sheltered through credentialing and licensing (e.g., doctors, professors, lawyers, medical technicians) and, on the other, occupations with little worker protection (e.g., office clericals, nonoffice clericals, service workers). Thus, sheltering is likely to obtain only for special categories of workers in this industrial group.

When we turn to an analysis of females, we observe roughly the same ranking among industries as for males, but slightly lower percentages of stayers in all industry categories except "other services." Presumably, women are less closely tied to their industries because occupational specialization, largely as office clericals and officer workers, is less industry-specific (women in these occupations can shift more readily among industries) and because pay inducements to remain are smaller. The relatively high percentage of stayers in other services very likely reflects the higher importance of industry-specific occupations (e.g., nurses, medical technicians, paralegals).

It is interesting to observe how the percentage of stayers is affected by recessions. Declines are observed in every industry category for both males and females (except TCU for females). Here we see the effect of layoffs under conditions of corporate retrenchment and declining employment.

An intriguing paradox is that long-term adverse conditions in the labor market may act to cause workers to remain in old jobs

Table 4.11   Percentage of Male and Female Stayers Relative to Initial Covered Workforce in Each Industry, Average for Seven SMSAs, 1971–1973 and 1973–1975

| | Males | | | |
| | 1971–1973 | | 1973–1975 | |
	Average[a]	Range	Average[a]	Range
All industries	55.6	50.4–66.6	48.9	44.4–64.4
Construction	49.7	41.4–63.0	43.0	39.1–51.7
Manufacturing	59.4	48.9–71.7	53.7	44.4–75.5
TCU	68.1	62.1–74.0	61.9	53.9–70.2
Wholesale/Retail	51.5	45.4–54.8	45.0	41.6–49.1
FIRE	55.0	50.5–64.3	48.1	34.5–63.9
Other services	53.0	47.0–59.2	49.0	42.8–56.0

| | Females | | | |
| | 1971–1973 | | 1973–1975 | |
	Average[a]	Range	Average[a]	Range
All industries	53.7	47.3–61.0	48.8	43.3–57.8
Construction	41.9	28.6–55.6	41.1	33.9–63.1
Manufacturing	57.6	39.1–64.1	48.2	33.9–63.1
TCU	64.6	31.9–68.4	67.0	54.4–78.1
Wholesale/Retail	47.7	39.9–68.4	40.7	36.6–48.9
FIRE	51.7	45.9–59.6	50.3	32.8–60.3
Other services	56.8	49.5–65.1	54.9	46.5–65.6

[a]Modified average: highest and lowest values have been dropped. Percentages for males and females computed separately relative to their respective initial covered workforce in each industry.

Source: U.S. Bureau of Economic Analysis, *Ten Percent Continuous Work History Sample.*

because openings in other industries simply do not occur in large numbers. In Buffalo, the metropolitan area with the lowest rate of overall employment growth during the period 1971–1975, percentages of stayers were highest among the seven SMSAs in all industries except wholesale-retail, for both males and females (see Table 5.6 below).

NEW ENTRANTS

The most striking observation regarding work opportunities for first-job seekers is the variation among places in the size of the flow of all new entrants relative to the size of the workforce (Table 4.12). In fast-growing places like Phoenix and Denver, the percentage is quite high, roughly one-fourth for males during the period 1971–1973, and about 40 percent for females.* For the declining Buffalo economy it is very low, 15 percent for males, 30 percent for females. For the remaining places the percentages lie largely in the intermediate range.

One might suppose, a priori, that the relative importance of new entrants would decline at some point as the rate of growth increases, since new entrants are presumably drawn from the local resident population. Fast growth might be expected to exhaust rather quickly the local supply of young, first-job applicants (newly arriving families would not be expected to contribute significantly to the supply since, being young on average, they tend to be childless or to have small children) and to increase reliance upon migrants to fill job vacancies.

Table 4.12 indicates that this is not the case. The supply of new entrants appears to be extremely flexible. It seems, therefore, that many young people in the slow-growing places, who would have taken jobs if growth rates were high, simply do not find employment.

A second finding relates to entry points within the employment system (Table 4.13). It is wholesale-retail, other services, and manufacturing that constitute the major entry points. Wholesale-retail and other services together account for 57 percent of male entries and 71 percent of female entries, shares which are for the most part disproportionately large when related to these categories' shares of total industrial employment. Manufacturing varies sharply in terms of its relative importance in the industrial structure of places and thus in the share of inflows accounted for by new entrants. Yet, in most places manufacturing remains an

---

*The female new entrant flow tends to overstate the number of women entering the job market for the first time. Women often withdraw from employment and return several years later, appearing as new entrants in the latest time period studied. Men tend to enter employment only once or to leave for only short periods.

Table 4.12   **Percentage of New Entrants and Inmigrants Relative to Final Covered Workforce, Seven SMSAs, 1971–1973**

	New entrants[a]		Inmigrants[a]	
	Male	Female	Male	Female
Atlanta	18.0	32.8	14.7	12.3
Denver	25.0	40.2	17.5	14.2
Buffalo	14.6	29.7	5.7	5.0
Phoenix	26.5	39.4	18.8	13.2
Columbus	20.3	36.0	18.6	9.8
Nashville	20.6	31.4	12.4	8.6
Charlotte	17.7	28.3	17.2	11.0
Modified average	17.0	33.9	16.1	11.0

[a]Percentages for males and females computed separately relative to their respective 1973 covered employment.

Source: U.S. Bureau of Economic Analysis, *Ten Percent Continuous Work History Sample.*

important entry point for young workers, even though it typically receives a much smaller share of new entrants than its share of total employment.

How are we to assess the earnings prospects of new entrants in those industries which receive the lion's share of young job seekers? Our earlier analysis shows that many sectors of manufacturing offer largely middle-range incomes as the ultimate job prospect, and that in these sectors young men, and to a much lesser extent young women, have reason to expect to attain such earnings in time. The prospects for entrants in wholesale-retail and in other services are less promising. In wholesale-retail (largely retail), the national and the seven SMSA data reveal that very few well-paid jobs exist. In other services there are a restricted number of very well-paid jobs, but these are largely available to those with special training as professionals or technicians.

It appears, therefore, that in the services, upward mobility depends heavily on opportunities to advance through change in

Table 4.13 Average Distributions of 1973 Covered Workforce and 1971–1973 Flows of New Entrants, Job In-Movers and Job Out-Movers among Industries, Males and Females (in percentages) Average for Seven SMSAs

	1973 Covered workforce	1971–1973 New entrants	1971–1973 Job movers in[a]	1971–1973 Job movers out[b]	Entrance to exit ratio Col. 3 ÷ Col. 4
	(1)	(2)	(3)	(4)	(5)
Males					
Construction	12.3	13.2	17.3	10.3	1.7
Manufacturing	30.1	20.7	22.0	29.0	0.8
TCU	8.2	4.0	8.6	5.6	1.5
Wholesale/Retail	27.6	37.0	24.6	32.5	0.8
FIRE	6.2	5.5	8.5	5.3	1.6
Other services	15.3	20.2	18.4	17.6	1.1
Females					
Construction	1.4	1.3	3.0	2.9	1.0
Manufacturing	19.4	15.3	19.2	16.5	1.2
TCU	4.2	2.5	4.7	3.5	1.3
Wholesale/Retail	28.9	36.5	24.6	35.4	0.7
FIRE	9.7	8.1	15.5	10.9	1.4
Other services	35.0	34.8	33.1	27.9	1.2

[a]"Job movers in" shows destination of job change of stayers who moved across industry lines.
[b]"Job movers out" shows industry of origin of job change of stayers who moved across industry lines.

Note: All data shown are modified averages for seven places with highest and lowest values dropped. Percentages do not add to 100.

Source: U.S. Bureau of Economic Analysis, *Ten Percent Continuous Work History Sample.*

employment involving movement among industries, in search of opportunities for better pay and terms of employment.

JOB MOVERS

Some evidence regarding such opportunities may be gleaned from analysis of the flows of job movers. Table 4.13 presents distributions of male and female job movers among the industry groups into which they have transferred (job in-movers) along with distributions of these workers in terms of the industries from which they have departed (job out-movers). *

The principal finding seems to be that there is quite a lot of moving about of workers among industries. To be sure there is a substantial net exodus of men and women from wholesale-retail. Yet nowhere is there a one-way street. Wholesale-retail absorbs a fourth of both male and female inmovers; other services, 18 percent of males and 33 percent of females. Construction and TCU, which typically offer better-than-average earnings for men and have quite favorable entrance-to-exit ratios (column 5), nevertheless account for only a fourth of all male job inmovers. The evidence, though indirect, points to the general conclusion that there do not seem to be a great many opportunities for advancement simply through job-hopping. The problem is likely to be particularly troublesome in those labor markets in which the rate of growth is low and in which the retailing and consumer services sectors are relatively large. This will be particularly true for women and minority workers, who tend to be stuck with those jobs having restricted opportunity for improvement.

Conclusion

In this chapter, we have begun to investigate the extent to which certain characteristics of work, which are developing as a result of the economy's shift to the services, are emerging in the seven metropolitan labor markets under study, and to analyze their implications for employment opportunities for different classes of workers.

*The lack of coverage of the public sector is particularly troublesome here. It is in the public sector that many of the better-than-average jobs are located (see Table 3.3).

A general conclusion of this chapter is that growth and the industry mix of the metropolitan economy appear to hold major keys to opportunities for work. When growth occurs, shortages develop across the spectrum of occupations and open up new niches, some of which are appropriate for new workers (new entrants into the labor force or workers relocating from other metropolitan labor markets) and others which are hopefully better suited and more rewarding to the talents of workers already established in the labor force.

But the industry mix of places seems important regardless of growth, particularly as the employment base of metropolitan economies continues to shift from goods- to service-producing activities. Where the service industries that develop are characterized by a large number of firms of the sort that provide sheltering and promotion from within, an important segment of the workforce may expect to find a relatively favorable outlook in terms of both job security and advancement, and there are at least some attractive openings for younger workers as older workers retire. On the other hand, where developing service industries provide little sheltering, limited hierarchical structuring within firms and/or where there is little growth, workers seem to face bleak career prospects. These general tendencies appear confirmed by one of our general findings, which indicates that, however limited the opportunities, both new and established workers are continuously trying to enter the best paid and best sheltered industries.

Overall, this chapter seems to confirm many of the findings derived in the previous chapter from an analysis of the nation's data. Thus, the shift of metropolitan places toward service-oriented economies is seen to be accompanied by a steady increase in the number and shares of both white and minority female workers in their labor force, although for the most part in low or very low-paid jobs. Furthermore, trend analysis indicates very restricted historical improvement in the relative position of these female workers vis-à-vis their white male counterparts. Preliminary investigation of the data for the seven SMSAs also indicates that the transition at work is largely bypassing black male workers.

In the next two chapters, we attempt to clarify some of these findings through a detailed analysis of the changes occuring within the seven metropolitan labor markets.

CHAPTER 5

Seven Metropolitan Labor Markets
in Transition

The analysis presented thus far has demonstrated that observations at the national level regarding certain characteristics associated with individual service and nonservice industries tend to be applicable for individual metropolitan labor markets.

In this chapter and the one that follows, we determine the extent to which metropolitan labor markets may differ by examining selected evidence relating to the seven SMSAs chosen for study. The analysis falls into four sections, of which the first two, Growth and Industrial Transformation of Employment and Profiles of Seven Metropolitan Economies, are presented in this chapter, and the second two, Differences in Earnings of Various Worker Groups and Variations in Worker Mobility Patterns, in Chapter 6.

It is useful to observe at the outset that differences among metropolitan labor markets may arise from a number of factors, of which the following four are critical:

differences in the industry mix of places, as measured by the distribution of employment among industries;

differences in the extent to which fast-growing places create more opportunities for entering or moving through the local labor market than do those experiencing slow growth;

differences in the structure of individual industries in terms of the extent to which they are dominated by corporate employers who provide for a high degree of sheltering (usually large and/or union-dominated companies), or, alternatively, by firms that offer relatively unprotected jobs (usually small and/or nonunionized firms); and

differences in the functional missions of the establishments that characterize the industries that are represented in the locale and tend to affect occupational composition and earnings distribution. Here we are interested especially in observing the extent to which the establishments in question are engaged in the delivery of services (i.e., headquarters, credit-processing) as contrasted with direct production of goods.

Variations in the industry mix and in growth rates are easiest to measure and provide a point of departure for understanding the nature of individual metropolitan economies. They are studied in the present chapter by analysis of the detailed *County Business Patterns* employment data rather than the coarser Social Security materials. As indicated in Chapter 2, differences in the industry mix of places are in part determined by the variations in functional roles of individual SMSAs within the larger urban system. Moreover, the economic history of a city places a heavy stamp on the mix of businesses and industries.

Variations among places in corporate structure and in the functional missions of establishments within given industries are more difficult to study. They can be partially identified by means of less conventional statistical sources (business directories, directories of local Chamber of Commerce, etc.), which provide some indication of the extent to which a particular industry is dominated by a few large corporate institutions as opposed to a multitude of small firms; is likely to be unionized; or is represented by headquarters, divisional offices, or other administrative facilities, as opposed to production establishments.

In the section that follows, we deal with growth and changing industrial mix of employment. The next section, Profiles, inquires into all four sources of variation stated above. Individual place descriptions are neither systematic nor exhaustive; they do, however, make use of pertinent information gleaned from various sources to sketch the principal characteristics of the economy of each SMSA.

Growth and Industrial
Transformation of Employment

POPULATION AND EMPLOYMENT GROWTH TRENDS

Table 5.1 presents the seven SMSAs in order of their 1976 population size and indicates population and employment growth experience during two periods — 1960–1970 and 1970–1976. In terms of the size hierarchy of places used in our discussion of Chapter 2, the 1976 population figures indicate that the five largest places (respectively Atlanta, Denver, Buffalo, Phoenix, and Columbus) fall within the bottom half of the first tier of the urban hierarchy (Size 2 SMSAs), while Nashville and Charlotte fall within the upper half of the second tier (Size 3 SMSAs) (see Table 2.3). On average, those SMSAs commonly regarded as part of the Sunbelt urban system have experienced higher rates of population growth than their two northern counterparts (Buffalo and Columbus), but it is worth noting that Columbus held its own well, despite its location in a region under stress.

In terms of employment growth, all places have exhibited slower average annual rates of growth during the 1970s than during the 1960s — not unlike the overall tendencies for the nation. Still, all of the places except Buffalo have grown faster than the nation over the entire seventeen-year span. Indeed, Phoenix, Denver, and Atlanta are among some of the fastest-growing SMSAs in the entire nation. The pronounced tendency for employment to grow more rapidly than population in both periods can be explained largely by increased labor force participation, related to the entry into the job market of large numbers of mature women and of the baby boom generation.

It is also interesting to observe the variations in 1976 ratios of employment to population. The low ratios found in Phoenix and Buffalo are probably due to very different causes: in Phoenix, a higher-than-average population of retirees,* and in Buffalo, severely restricted job opportunities for new entrants (see below).

---

*For the record, the same low ratio is found among quite a number of southern SMSAs essentially for the same reason: their role as retirement centers.

Table 5.1 Population and Employment, 1976, and Growth in Population and Employment, 1960s and 1970s, in Seven SMSAs and the United States

| | Population[a] | | | Employment[a] | | | Ratio: Employment to population |
| | Average annual rate of growth | | Number (in thousands) | Average annual rate of growth | | Number (in thousands) | |
	1960–1970	1970–1976	1976	1959–1969	1969–1976	1976	1976
Atlanta	3.1	2.0	1,804.8	5.3	3.0	775.6	43.0
Denver	2.8	2.5	1,438.4	4.7	4.6	615.4	42.8
Buffalo	0.3	-0.2	1,328.0	1.8	-0.6	466.0	35.1
Phoenix	3.8	4.0	1,224.1	6.4	5.4	437.6	35.7
Columbus	1.8	0.8	1,072.0	3.7	1.8	440.6	41.1
Nashville	1.5	1.4	763.5	4.7	3.3	327.4	42.9
Charlotte	2.3	1.0	593.0	4.9	2.6	295.3	49.8
United States	1.3	0.9	215,200.0	3.2	1.8	77,660.2	36.7

[a] All figures are shown on the basis of the 1976 geographical definition of the Seven SMSAs.

Source: U.S. Statistical Abstract, 1979. County Business Patterns, 1959, 1969, 1976 and Employment and Earnings, 1959, 1969, 1976 (see Appendix Table 3).

THE EMPLOYMENT TRANSFORMATION

Tables 5.2 and 5.3 present evidence pertaining to the transformation of the economic base of these seven places during the 1959–1976 period. The first of these two tables summarizes an analysis of all job increases and job decreases in each major industrial sector during the two periods under consideration. (For an explanation of method and a more detailed presentation see Appendix Table 3).

Only job increases are shown in this summary table. During the 1960s job decreases (for both the nation and the seven places) were insignificant relative to job increases, and during the 1970s job decreases, though sizable were overwhelmingly concentrated in the manufacturing sector where job increases in certain subindustries were typically washed out by job decreases in others. This is made clear in Table 5.2, in which we have indicated whether the manufacturing sector experienced a net job increase (noted by JI in parentheses) or a net job decrease (noted by JD in parentheses). With this added specification, the summary distribution of job increases is a valid, simplified way of looking at the overall transformation of these economies through the most recent period.

During the 1959–1969 period, the magnitude of the transformation to the services undergone by the seven places was evidenced by the fact that, on the average, the share of job increases in manufacturing (Table 5.2) was much smaller than the comparable share of employment at the beginning of the period (Table 5.3), while for services as a whole the share of job increases was much larger. Only in Phoenix was the share of job increases in manufacturing sizeably greater than its comparable share of employment at the beginning of the period. In terms of industrial transformation, important gains were reported in the complex of corporate activities (central administrative offices and producer services combined — see Chapter 2, second section), in the nonprofit services, and in government, the shares of job increases being in almost every comparison larger than the employment shares of the respective sectors at the beginning of the period.

The most significant difference between the 1969–1976 period and the earlier 1959–1969 period stems from the shift from growth to stagnation or decline of manufacturing employment in almost

Table 5.2 Distribution of Job Increases among Major Industry Groups: United States, Seven SMSAs, and Modified Average for the Seven SMSAs, 1959-1969 and 1969-1976 (in percentages)

	1959-1969									1969-1976								
	United States	Atlanta	Denver	Buffalo	Phoenix	Columbus	Nashville	Charlotte	Modified average	United States	Atlanta	Denver	Buffalo	Phoenix	Columbus	Nashville	Charlotte	Modified average
Construction	3.6	7.5	4.4	0.7	1.9	4.2	7.3	5.4	4.6	2.4	0.4	7.3	2.1	4.9	0.0	1.7	7.3	4.0
Manufacturing[a]	18.7	16.0	15.9	16.3	30.4	17.8	22.0	28.5	20.1	2.6	4.5	10.0	11.0	8.6	7.2	11.2	11.3	9.6
										(JD)	(JD)	(JI)	(JD)	(JD)	(JD)	(JI)	(JD)	
Distributive service	8.0	17.1	9.3	4.7	6.8	6.2	8.1	15.6	9.2	6.8	12.7	10.5	2.2	9.7	8.8	13.1	26.3	11.0
Complex of corporate activities	19.1	20.0	17.0	19.1	14.3	21.3	18.6	20.6	19.1	24.9	35.9	24.0	24.7	20.8	28.0	20.5	21.7	23.8
Retail service	14.7	14.2	18.6	17.1	16.5	16.3	12.8	10.8	15.4	19.2	16.7	17.6	13.3	21.2	22.2	14.3	10.3	16.6
Mainly consumer services	4.1	4.4	4.7	2.8	4.9	3.9	3.5	3.5	4.0	4.1	7.1	3.7	5.4	5.5	3.4	5.4	2.9	4.7
Nonprofit	9.6	5.1	9.5	9.0	7.4	6.4	9.9	1.9	7.5	13.1	6.6	6.3	20.0	6.6	12.4	12.6	6.0	8.9
Government	21.9	15.5	19.3	29.9	17.1	23.6	17.5	13.4	18.6	25.3	16.0	18.7	21.4	22.2	17.4	20.8	13.5	18.9

[a] Total job decreases in all industries during the period 1959-1969 were insignificant. Job decreases during the period 1969-1976 were substantial and primarily concentrated in the manufacturing sector. Net declines (JD) or net increases (JI) in manufacturing jobs are indicated in parentheses below the share of job increases.

Note: Share of job increases accounted for by agriculture and mining is not shown.

Source: Based on Appendix Table 3.

Table 5.3 Distribution of Employment among Major Industry Groups, United States, Seven SMSAs, and Modified Average for the Seven SMSAs, 1959 and 1976 (in percentages)

	1959									1976								
	United States	Atlanta	Denver	Buffalo	Phoenix	Columbus	Nashville	Charlotte	Modified average	United States	Atlanta	Denver	Buffalo	Phoenix	Columbus	Nashville	Charlotte	Modified average
Construction	5.0	5.5	6.3	4.2	9.8	4.7	6.2	7.3	6.0	4.4	5.0	6.2	3.3	5.7	3.7	5.6	7.0	5.2
Manufacturing	31.7	26.3	19.3	41.7	18.7	30.0	28.5	34.8	27.8	22.9	14.9	14.2	27.8	15.8	19.4	22.1	26.1	19.7
Distributive services	11.9	17.0	16.0	11.3	14.0	10.8	13.2	19.4	14.3	10.4	16.8	12.9	9.8	10.7	9.5	12.0	20.3	12.4
Complex of corporate activities	10.3	12.1	13.0	8.6	11.1	12.2	10.7	9.4	11.1	14.7	21.0	17.5	13.1	16.0	18.0	15.1	15.5	16.4
Retail services	15.3	15.3	15.8	14.9	17.6	15.8	15.1	13.4	15.4	16.0	15.5	17.3	16.4	19.3	17.4	14.5	12.2	16.2
Mainly consumer services	4.5	5.0	5.2	3.6	7.3	4.1	5.2	4.7	4.8	4.3	5.4	4.7	3.9	6.2	4.1	4.6	4.0	4.6
Nonprofit	3.5	2.9	4.7	3.6	3.2	3.0	5.3	2.9	3.5	6.5	4.7	6.6	6.9	5.9	5.9	8.0	3.4	6.0
Government	16.3	15.5	19.0	11.9	17.9	19.0	15.3	7.9	15.9	19.5	16.5	19.4	18.6	19.9	21.5	17.7	11.1	18.4

Note: Share of employment accounted for by agriculture and mining is not shown.

Source: Based on Appendix Table 3.

every SMSA and the nation as well. For both the nation and the seven places, the major gains during this latter period, as measured by shares of job increases, were in the complex of corporate activities, retail services, and government.

Table 5.3, which shows the employment shares of the major industry groupings in the seven places at the beginning and end of the 1959–1976 period, summarizes the combined effects of these various trends. Among the five largest places, four—Atlanta, Denver, Phoenix, Columbus, but excluding Buffalo—appear to have developed strong complexes of corporate activities, while the role played by the distributive services in these economies has declined slightly in relative importance, at least in employment terms. This general trend is very much like that demonstrated by other regional nodal places of similar size, as described in Chapter 2.

There are also indications that other sectors exert, though more selectively, an important influence in these five larger places. Manufacturing still accounts for a fifth of total employment in Columbus. Retailing has increased its share of employment significantly in Denver, Phoenix, and Columbus. Finally, government plays a fairly important role among these larger places, especially in Denver, Phoenix, and Columbus. Curiously, government is least important in Atlanta, even though this major southern city is a state capital.

Buffalo stands in sharp contrast to the four other larger places. It has been characterized by a fast-declining, though still large, manufacturing sector and a certain inability to counterbalance this decline by a vigorous growth in export-oriented services. Although Buffalo has increased the share of its employment in the complex of corporate activities during the period, this appears to reflect simply the transformation of activities within corporations that have long been major factors in the economy of the immediate region. In the end, the share of its complex of corporate activities remains markedly lower than that of the four other places examined so far and even that of Nashville and Charlotte. Moreover, Buffalo has seemed unable to hold on to its distributive sectors, losing part of its wholesale and transportation traffic to other ports on the St. Lawrence Seaway (such as Montreal). As a result, a significant part of Buffalo's transformation to the services has come about with the growth of more residentiary services, especially retailing, nonprofit, and local government. Briefly, Buffalo's experience over the seventeen-year period is not unlike that suggested in Chapter 2, which described a number of large or medium-sized manufacturing-type places which are undergoing a very difficult process of change.

Nashville and Charlotte, which are relatively smaller, have demonstrated yet a different pattern of transformation. Both places have maintained a very strong distributive service sector, unusually so in the case of Charlotte. They have both made substantial gains in their complex of corporate activities, although their share of the sector remains lower than that of the larger places (except for Buffalo) at the end of the period. In this respect, both places follow the pattern of smaller size, subregional nodal places described in Chapter 2, whose strength seems to lie primarily in their ability to distribute goods and to provide services within their immediate region.

Still, the two places differ in certain respects. The Charlotte SMSA, with little strength in nonprofit services and government, is strongly oriented toward manufactures, although the city of Charlotte itself is predominantly service-oriented. Nashville, for its part, has preserved its lead in the nonprofit sector (education and medical) and found major employment and income-generating strength as the seat of state government. Its manufacturing sector, though important, is considerably smaller in relative terms.

This first impressionistic picture of the seven metropolitan labor markets points out some major differences in the way they have transformed in the course of the last two decades. While the patterns identified so far are consistent with the general presentation of Chapter 2, a closer look beneath the crust of the very general typology outlined earlier indicates some substantial variations even among places of similar type and size. What remains to be discussed is the differing balance in the industrial structure of each place and its impact on the mix of "good" and "bad" jobs.

The quality of employment is, as noted earlier, partly a function of the occupational structure of each industry, but it is also the result of other attributes that vary from place to place. The roles played by large national and international corporations, by large regional corporations, and by small local firms, unions, and other institutional factors are important.

In the seven profiles that follow, we highlight industrial structure and important institutional characteristics of each place in
order to provide additional clues as to the true nature of these
seven labor markets.

Profiles of Seven Metropolitan Economies

A simple way to summarize and highlight the industrial structure
of each SMSA is to make use of location quotients. By normalizing to the nation's average the employment share of each industry
in each place, location quotients encompass in a single measure
the relative standing of each sector. These quotients have been
compiled for all seven places for a detailed breakdown of industries (Table 5.4). Quite logically, they confirm the findings
derived from Tables 5.2 and 5.3. They are used here along with
such other information as could be gleaned from various sources
(Fortune Magazine, 1961; Dun and Bradstreet, 1976; Marketing
Economics Institute, 1976; National Register, 1976; as well as the
individual directories published by the Chambers of Commerce of
each of the seven places) to sketch the basic characteristics of each
metropolitan economy.

ATLANTA

The most outstanding feature of Atlanta's recent transformation is
the strengthening of its role as a major, regional, nodal center. In
terms of employment shares, the location quotients presented in
Table 5.4 speak for themselves. With 1976 location quotients of
165.0 in TCU, 157.0 in wholesale, and 142.0 in the complex of
corporate activities, Atlanta exhibits nodal tendencies much
stronger than any of the six other places studied (with the exception of Charlotte's strength in the distributive services).

In 1976, Atlanta was host to four of the Fortune 500 firms
(Coca Cola, Gold Kist, National Service Industries, and Sim-
mons), four of the Fortune Transportation-Retail-Utilities 150
and nine of the Second Fortune 500 industrial firms. Yet, these
measures are by no means fully representative of Atlanta's
strength as a corporate center. Its strength seems to be best
highlighted by the number of very large corporations that have

opened divisional head offices in Atlanta (roughly one hundred divisions of 55 of the Fortune 500), regional sales headquarters and field offices. By the Atlanta Chamber of Commerce's own count, as of 1976, 439 of the Fortune 500 had some kind of presence in the Atlanta SMSA, as well as 46 of the 50 largest insurance companies, 45 of the 50 largest transportation companies, 35 of the 50 largest diversified financial companies, and 28 of the 50 largest retailing companies. In short, by the mid-1970s, Atlanta had come to be looked upon by the larger corporations as *the* major center for operations in the southeastern regional markets — a function the city is now trying to expand by becoming an active trading center with Central America. It is worth noting that this latter development has been helped by the expansion of Atlanta's international air routes to countries in that region.

An additional and meaningful measure of Atlanta's emerging role as a major regional center is that it is one of the few metropolitan centers where the very large commercial banks (located in New York, Chicago, San Francisco, and Los Angeles) have opened Edge Act Corporations and Loan Production Offices.* These facilities have come to reinforce the banking capacity of Atlanta, whose own banks, albeit fairly large, have traditionally been more locally oriented.

Atlanta's relative strength in TCU is perhaps most outstanding in air transportation. It has a large international airport and is the major base of operations for Delta, one of the largest airlines in the nation (Delta has well over 8,000 employees in the Atlanta SMSA). Yet it is also an important center in trucking, in utilities (Georgia Power and Light employs over 5,000 in the SMSA), and in communications (Southern Bell Telephone is headquartered in the SMSA, as is Continental Telephone). Moreover, in dollar volume Atlanta ranks as the ninth-largest wholesale center in the nation, specializing in the distribution of motor vehicles, electrical goods, and hardware supply and machinery.

The importance of nodal functions in Atlanta's economic base may tend to underemphasize the fact that Atlanta is also the state capital (with a resulting sizeable federal and state bureaucratic

---

*Edge Act Corporations are banking subsidiaries dealing exclusively with foreign investment and trade financing. In the absence of interstate banking, loan production offices have been set up very selectively by the very large banks in key cities as a means to channel new loan business back to the home office.

Table 5.4 1959 and 1976 Location Quotients of Employment in Major Industry Groups, Seven SMSAs

	Atlanta		Denver		Buffalo	
	1959	1976	1959	1976	1959	1976
Agriculture, extractive, and transformative						
Mining	13.3	12.0	49.1	103.8	6.2	6.7
Construction	110.7	113.0	126.3	141.8	85.2	76.7
Manufacturing	84.0	65.0	59.7	62.1	132.1	121.7
Services						
Distributive services	143.0	160.9	135.0	123.3	96.1	93.3
TCU, of which	129.3	165.0	129.8	122.8	100.0	88.3
Air transportation	(345.3)	(573.0)	(371.9)	(312.6)	(44.0)	(55.0)
Communication	(117.3)	(101.0)	(143.9)	(131.7)	(84.0)	(73.3)
Wholesale	156.0	157.0	138.6	124.1	32.6	38.3
Complex of corporate activities	116.0	142.0	126.3	119.0	84.0	90.0
CAO & A	96.0	173.0	131.6	119.0	88.9	66.7
FIRE	126.7	136.0	129.8	120.3	74.0	80.0
Banking	(92.0)	(105.0)	(100.0)	(97.5)	(100.0)	(113.3)
Insurance	(162.7)	(146.0)	(129.8)	(98.7)	(67.9)	(75.0)
Real estate	(96.0)	(171.0)	(126.3)	(141.8)	(59.3)	(60.0)
Corporate services	112.0	134.0	121.1	117.7	93.8	108.3
Retail services	100.0	97.0	103.5	107.6	95.5	101.7
Mainly consumer services	113.3	126.0	114.1	110.1	80.3	90.0
Nonprofit services	79.9	71.4	134.5	100.9	103.5	106.4
Health	64.0	62.0	135.1	105.1	105.0	110.0
Education	140.0	111.0	128.1	87.4	100.0	93.0
Government	96.0	85.0	115.8	100.0	74.1	95.0

Source: Based on Appendix Table 3.

Table 5.4 (continued)

Phoenix		Columbus		Nashville		Charlotte	
1959	1976	1959	1976	1959	1976	1959	1976
12.5	16.1	14.8	21.0	24.2	19.1	6.5	7.9
200.0	130.4	94.5	82.5	124.2	128.6	145.2	157.9
59.4	69.6	96.3	84.2	90.9	97.6	109.7	113.2
118.8	102.0	92.0	91.5	111.8	115.2	163.3	194.2
109.9	89.3	87.0	82.5	93.9	109.5	148.4	223.7
(81.3)	(87.5)	(29.6)	(26.3)	84.9	(64.3)	(80.7)	(110.5)
(146.9)	(105.4)	(88.9)	(101.8)	(124.2)	(138.1)	(106.5)	(100.0)
128.1	114.3	96.3	98.3	127.3	121.4	177.4	168.4
109.4	108.9	114.8	122.8	100.0	102.4	90.3	105.3
31.3	69.6	94.5	128.1	90.9	114.3	93.5	121.1
134.4	125.0	109.3	121.1	118.2	107.1	106.5	110.5
(125.0)	(107.1)	70.4	77.2	(100.0)	(100.0)	(90.3)	(126.3)
(131.3)	(110.7)	111.1	208.8	(127.3)	(147.6)	(135.5)	(118.4)
(162.5)	(142.9)	83.3	114.1	(72.7)	(85.7)	(77.4)	(81.6)
106.3	110.7	131.4	121.1	84.9	92.9	67.7	94.7
115.6	121.4	103.7	108.8	100.0	90.5	87.1	76.3
162.5	144.6	96.3	93.0	133.3	107.2	103.2	92.1
91.5	90.5	84.2	90.7	150.3	122.5	81.3	51.5
100.0	100.0	88.9	96.5	90.9	109.5	83.8	52.6
62.5	51.8	64.8	63.2	363.6	183.3	64.5	50.0
112.5	110.7	116.7	110.5	90.9	90.5	48.4	57.9

complex) and an important educational center (Georgia Tech, Georgia State University, and Emory University). The reader will note also from Table 5.4 that Atlanta's mainly consumer services tend to be above average, partly because of its hotel facilities (largely related to convention activity and the needs of traveling businessmen).

One of the consequences of this dramatic move into the services has been a no less sizeable decline of the relative importance of manufacturing in Atlanta's economy: from 26 percent of employment in the sector in 1959 to a mere 15 percent in 1976. Atlanta's manufacturing is essentially characterized by one large employing sector in the high-paying industries, transportation equipment, and several smaller but sizeable ones in the low-paying industries: textile, apparel, furniture, paper, and printing. Chemicals and building product firms are also important employers. General Motors and the Ford Motor Company are the two largest employers in the transportation equipment sector, with Lockheed Georgia coming next. In textile, apparel, furniture, and paper, the presence of large corporations varies to a considerable degree, depending on the structure of the specific industry.

Although the above profile depicts Atlanta as a thriving regional center, in fact its postwar economic history has not been free from conflict and major social problems. As a former leading city of the old South, it has inherited problems associated with a large black population. Thus, a major question to be raised in assessing Atlanta's future is whether or not the transformation toward a greater role for services provides an effective route toward integrating the area's minority population into the economic structure.

DENVER

Sustained rapid growth has positioned Denver as the key nodal center in the Mountain States region. Building on its earlier strengths as a major distribution center and a center of government (Denver is also a state capital), Denver has succeeded in recent years in attracting a variety of large and very large companies that have set up headquarters or divisional head offices in that locale. This influx has been helped since 1973 by major developments in the national economy.

Following the energy crisis, major U.S. energy firms have invested heavily in oil and gas exploration in Colorado and Wyoming, and in the mining of coal, uranium, and other minerals in these and other western states as well. In the process, many of the major U.S. oil and energy firms—for example, Gulf, Occidental Petroleum, Marathon Oil, and Phelps Dodge—have opened major divisional or regional headquarters in Denver, from which they can oversee their field operations. Similar moves having been made by a number of firms in the mining machinery and drilling equipment field, the immediate result has been a major office building construction boom in Denver's downtown and the creation of large numbers of jobs by energy firms (largely in administration-related activities) and closely linked producer service firms. A recent report by the Colorado Energy Research Institute estimates that, as of 1979, there were 866 firms employing close to 12,000 workers in the SMSA that were directly engaged in energy exploration and production, and an additional 1,200 firms employing another 12,000 workers in closely linked activities (such as geology, mine engineering and construction, equipment manufacturing, etc.) (Colorado Energy Research Institute, 1979, p. 15).

While this development has contributed a great deal to the growth of the Denver SMSA during the 1970s, many observers of the local scene are quick to point out that its leveling off may be imminent.* Now that the basic administrative and producer service-related infrastructure is in place, job creation by the energy firms has begun shifting to the fields (mostly in Wyoming or other parts of Colorado) where the drilling and mining takes place.

Denver's role as an insurance center is not outstanding, and its banking tends to remain primarily regional in scope.† While this is not to say that these two sectors have been totally unaffected by Denver's growth in the energy field, it does point to the fact that for a number of reasons the major energy firms seem to have largely bypassed the local financial community.** Denver does show, however, some special strength in leasing (truck and

---

*This was confirmed by almost everyone whom we interviewed during our field visit.

†Possibly even more so than banking in places like Atlanta, Phoenix, or even Columbus.

**Apparently because of a strong self-financing capacity or the use of the services of money center banks by the large energy firms.

railroad cars) and as a head office location for several of the sub-sidiaries of the very large diversified financial firms.

In addition, Denver is an important transportation and whole-sale center. It has long enjoyed a strategic position within the western railroad network and now finds a new raison d'être for leadership in the increased importance of shipping of coal and minerals. The Union Pacific, the Colorado and Southern (a sub-sidiary of Burlington Northern), and the Denver and Rio Grande Western (a subsidiary of Rio Grande Industries) railroads are headquartered in the city. Denver is also important as a trucking center and is a major air transportation hub, with United, Western, Frontier, and Continental airlines having major routes running to, through, and from the city. Indeed, the latter phenomenon is not unrelated to the development of Denver as a preferred site for corporate offices. Denver's above-average wholesaling sector is strongly specialized in the trading of motor vehicles, electrical goods, and hardware supplies, and in machinery and equipment supply.

Denver's manufacturing sector is relatively small, with some special strengths in transportation equipment (aeronautics — e.g., Beech aircraft in Boulder), in machinery (both computer and machine tools — IBM employs 3,600 people in plants located in Boulder), in building products (including prefabricated materials), and in printing and publishing. Denver is also the home to Samsonite, the luggage manufacturer (a subsidiary of Beatrice Foods), which employs over 3,000 people in its Denver production facility.

The importance of Denver's relatively large retail consumer services and nonprofit sectors is related both to its vigorous and diversified service economy and to its role as a tourist center. Denver's early strength in tourism was undoubtedly a positive fac-tor since it contributed to the development of a large airport, which later strengthened its newer headquarters orientation.

In the end, while Denver has shown a certain capacity to make use of some of the local resources developed during earlier periods, one may question whether its recent economic growth, which has been built largely through a rapid influx of people and firms and only to a modest extent through a continuous building of local resources, is an entirely desirable development. As we shall see below, this development is not unlike that which has occurred in Phoenix, and is one which calls for some careful evaluation (see Chapter 7).

Buffalo remains essentially a two-industry town. It is a manufacturer of transportation equipment (mostly auto) and a producer of chemicals, with a large number of supplier firms depending on the livelihood of the former. In the mid 1970s, General Motors had five major facilities in the SMSA, employing close to 23,000, while Ford had one major establishment employing more than 5,000. The size of their supplier firms varied from the very large to the very small, while their activity included a wide range of products (tires, electronic equipment, clutches, machine tools for the shops). Steel manufacturers were usually among the largest supplier firms (Bethlehem Steel — 8,000 employees, Republic Steel — 2,600 employees) but others were also large. Another important employer in the transportation equipment sector was the Bell aerospace Division of Textron (1600 employees). In the chemical industry, Buffalo's SMSA is the home of Hooker Chemicals and Plastics and Carborundum Corp. (Both employ over 3500 each in their various facilities in the SMSA). Union Carbide, Dupont, and Allied Chemical also have large facilities. While this short description may not give a full picture of Buffalo's entire manufacturing base, it underlines two of its most basic structural problems. Buffalo's heavy dependence on two industries under stress — automobiles (partly because of the rise of foreign competition and partly because of the incapacity of domestic producers to respond to changing consumer demands) and chemicals (because its high, associated health costs on neighboring populations have made its presence strongly questioned) — does not augur well for the manufacturing future of the locale.

Buffalo is headquarters to only one Fortune 500 (Carborundum Corp) and one Second Fortune 500 firm (Robin Industries). Moreover, the number of divisional head offices located in the city is far from being commensurate with the SMSA's size rank in the hierarchy of cities. This is consistent with the tradition that Buffalo is largely a blue collar town with little to offer by way of service diversification. It is intriguing that Buffalo, nevertheless, remains the home of one of the largest commercial banks in the nation—Marine Midland, which is active not only regionwide but also nationally and internationally. Here we observe, apparently, a hangover from Buffalo's former prominence as the gateway city to the Great Lakes.

Finally, as was noted earlier in this chapter, Buffalo seems to have lost part of its former importance as a regional distribution center. Perhaps this is best exemplified by the loss of 2,500 jobs in water transportation, other transportation services (e.g., customs, freight forwarding), and trucking from 1969 to 1976. Roughly three-fourths of this employment loss was accounted for by trucking, an industrial category that grew sharply during these years in virtually every other SMSA.

To conclude, despite the importance of large manufacturing firms, Buffalo seems to have been singularly unsuccessful in moving its economy toward the development of corporate headquarters activities and supporting services, as did most of the metropolitan economies studied here or certain of its neighboring cities, such as Albany and Rochester (see Noyelle and Stanback, forthcoming).

PHOENIX

Phoenix appears to be three economies in one, with limited linkages among the three. The first Phoenix is the old Phoenix, that of the large agribusiness and natural resource companies: Talley Industries, Southwest Forest Industries, Arizona Colorado Cattle and Land, AZL Resources, etc. Their impact on Phoenix is important to understand. Although their operations are spread widely over the Southwest, Phoenix remains a favorite locale for the central administration of such firms. In addition, these firms have been able to use their early knowledge of the city to play an important role in the land development boom of the past twenty years. Lastly, their presence has historically contributed to the growth of a number of local banks, including Valley National Bank—one of the nation's top 50 commercial banks.

The second Phoenix is the most visible one. It is the Phoenix of the developers, the real estate agents, the home builders, the retirees, the older and younger workers who have flocked to the city over the last two or three decades. Phoenix enjoys a favorable image as a residential center and, as a result, has become characterized by an above-average development of its retail and mainly consumer service sectors.

The third Phoenix is that of the large national and international corporations, which have come to regard Phoenix as a favorable site — mostly for manufacturing production and, in more limited instances, for administration. Phoenix's manufacturing sector developed after the war as a center of operation for aeronautic firms linked to federal military contracts (first Garett Corporation, a subsidiary of Fortune 500 Signal Co., which builds guided missiles, and later on, Lockheed and UMC), for computer manufacturing and assembly (General Electric and, more recently, Honeywell), and for primary and fabricated metals (AT&T–Western Electric employs half of the workforce of these industries in a plant that produces telephone wire). But more recently and, in some ways, more importantly, Phoenix has become a major center for the production of semiconductors (with Motorola, which employs close to 15,000 people in three huge plants, accounting for roughly half of the SMSA's employment in this industry).

On the administrative side, Greyhound, its subsidiary, Armour Co., and a number of divisions of major firms have joined the large agribusiness and national resources companies mentioned earlier in setting up headquarters or head offices in the city. Phoenix is also active in the field of insurance (with several large insurance companies established in the city either through regional offices or subsidiaries) and of leasing (heavy equipment for construction and agribusiness).

As a center of distributive services Phoenix is not outstanding. Its transportation sector is rather small for a city of its size, and its strength in wholesaling rests on servicing its large retailing sector (strong wholesaling of groceries) and its electronic equipment manufacturing (strong wholesaling of electrical goods and hardware supplies).

In the end, one of the most striking features of Phoenix is that its economy has been built very rapidly, mostly by bringing in people and activities from the outside, rather than by building on the strengths of its local population and local firms. Because the large and very large firms that have favored Phoenix for both production and administration facilities appear to have moved in with already well-established networks of supplier firms, there does not seem to have been a strong stimulation of local entrepreneurship. Furthermore, the kind of manufacturing that has most successfully developed of late (semiconductor) has called for a largely unskilled labor force and has required a very limited investment in a local pool of trained workers. In these and other respects, linkages between large firms and the local economy have thus far remained rather weak. One manifestation of this weakness is found in the lack of desire and commitment on the part of the large semiconductor manufacturers to develop sizeable research, managerial, and administrative facilities in the area, which would bring better jobs into Phoenix. Another result is that, relative to its size, Phoenix is poorly endowed with the kind of structure of small and medium-size manufacturing or producer service firms that might contribute favorably to the stability of the local economy by making the large firms more dependent on local resources.* We return to these issues in Chapter 7.

COLUMBUS (OHIO)

Although located in the center of one of the oldest manufacturing states of the nation, Columbus appears to have proceeded quite successfully with a service transformation of its employment base. This is all the more noteworthy in light of the difficulties met by many of its metropolitan neighbors in the old industrial belt (e.g., Buffalo).

A possible explanation is that Columbus took an early lead in the service transformation because of its function as a state capital and its early development of a strong research orientation. At a time when both the federal-state government connection and R&D functions were increasing in importance for the large corporation, Columbus appeared to have been well positioned to gain an important share of the expansion of the central administrative and auxiliary establishments of large local firms and to propel the development of a number of associated corporate services.

---

*Local development planners whom we met with in Phoenix demonstrated a keen awareness of this issue and of the need to correct such shortcomings. There may be signs that their efforts to improve this situation are beginning to pay off. See, for example, "Arizona Proves Fertile Ground for Electronics," in *Business Week,* July 13, 1981, pp. 14–15.

By the mid-1970s, Columbus's strength as a nodal center was best exemplified by the relative importance of its complex of corporate activities. In addition to having been chosen by Borden, Inc., as the new home for the company's headquarters, Columbus (and its immediate periphery) was host to the headquarters of six others of the Fortune 1000 industrial corporations (Anchor-Hocking, Greif Bros., Lancaster Colony, Ranco, Buckeye International, and Worthington Industries). More important, perhaps, was a solid presence of divisional head offices of a large number of the Fortune firms, an outgrowth of Columbus's earlier, strong manufacturing capacity whereby large firms with production facilities in the area decided to expand their administrative units locally. Furthermore, a number of these divisions have set up research facilities in the area, thereby reinforcing a powerful research complex organized around institutions such as the Batelle Memorial Institute (2,900 employees), the Chemical Abstracts Service (1,200 employees), and Ohio State University.

Despite the presence of BancOhio (one of the nation's top 50 bank holding companies), Columbus's banking sector remains relatively restricted. On the other hand, Columbus has been particularly successful in attracting insurance companies: it is now the home of Nation-wide Insurance (one of the nation's top 50 life insurers) and of a plethora of smaller-size companies, many of which are subsidiaries of some of the nation's largest ones.

Other examples of Columbus's successes in securing special niches for its complex of corporate activities are provided by the presence of the head offices of several fast food companies (White Castle, Wendy's, Arthur Treacher's, and Burger Chef) and of several large developers (e.g., Discovery Realty Trust Co.), which are active nationwide. All this provides evidence that Columbus has been able to develop the kind of specialized producer service firms capable of delivering services specially tailored to the needs of entrepreneurs in a variety of activities.

Columbus is the capital of Ohio, and state government is the largest employer in the SMSA (20,400 employees in 1976). As usually happens, a strong federal government presence (close to 12,000 employees) is associated with that of the state. In addition, the Columbus campus of the Ohio State University, one of the largest state university systems in the nation, employs slightly more than 16,000 people.

Trucking and communication (the Ohio Bell Telephone Co.

employs 5,000 people) are the mainstays of the Columbus TCU sector. Somewhat surprisingly, Columbus airport has remained relatively undersized, considering the functions the city is attempting to fulfill. The city is aware of its shortcoming and has plans well underway for a sizeable expansion of its facilities.

Although it has lost some of its former clout as a manufacturing center, Columbus has retained an important manufacturing base. Its strengths are in electrical machinery (Western Electric and Westinghouse account for a large share of the employment in the sector), machinery (with a substantial number of large firms engaged in manufacturing industrial machinery and equipment), transportation equipment (GM—Fisher Body Division has a facility that employs during peak periods close to 4,700 employees; Rockwell International—Aircraft division, 1,700 employees; and International Harvester, 1,500 employees), ordnance, and fabricated metals. In addition, Columbus is strong in chemicals, rubber and plastics, printing and instruments. Overall, these tend to be unionized and well paying industries. Yet, as the sizeable losses registered during the 1970s by the three largest manufacturing sectors (eletrical machinery, machinery, and transportation equipment) indicate, a major issue that the Columbus area must now face is whether the skill of its blue collar workforce can prevail over cost considerations and thereby permit Columbus to retain the best of its manufacturing sector.

Since many factors will surely influence the outcome, one cannot make a bold prediction as to what the future holds. Yet, Columbus's apparent success to date in managing its transformation in the face of adversity argues for following closely its future urban experience.

NASHVILLE

Nashville prides itself on being the cultural center of its region. But while everyone knows the city as the capital of country and western music, with its Grand Old Opry and its famous and less-than-famous recording stars, one is usually less aware of the importance of the city as a medical and educational center, as a center of government and, to a lesser extent, as a center for corporate administrative and financial activity.

As regards its role in education and health care, Nashville is home to two major southern universities, Vanderbilt (which employs 5,600 people in its educational and medical facilities) and Tennessee State (1,000 employees), and to several large hospitals. Moreover, Nashville's edge in medical facilities and in the medical professions seems to have opened the way for several, major, private hospital management corporations to set up head offices in the city (e.g., Hospital Corporation of America, which employs 2,000 locally, and General Care Corporation, 1,000).

In government, Nashville is the capital of one of the most rapidly growing states in the nation. In the late 1970s, there were more than 16,000 state government employees working in the city. Closely related was a significant federal government presence—more than 7,500 employees.

Nashville has developed as a center for corporate administrative and financial activity. While its banking institutions do not have the clout of those in Charlotte (see below), its insurance industry is of major importance. Nashville is the home of National Life and Accident Insurance Company, one of the nation's top 50 insurance companies, as well as host to the head offices of insurance subsidiaries of some of the largest insurance or financial companies (e.g., Life Casualty Insurance Co., a subsidiary of American General Insurance, one of the top 50 diversified financial companies).

On the industrial corporate administrative side, a number of firms engaged in the production of leather goods and apparel have chosen to locate high-echelon administrative units in the Nashville area. Genesco (a diversified apparel firm and one of the Fortune 500) has its headquarters in the city, as do the major divisions of several Fortune 500 firms specializing in one or more of these industries; e.g., Acme (a subsidiary of Northwest Industries, a Fortune 500), Genesco Shoe manufacturing Division, Georgia Boots (a division of U.S. Industries, a Fortune 500 firm), and Blue Bell Shoe Division.

On the production side, the most remarkable development in recent years is Nashville's steady buildup of sizable apparel, shoe, and furniture industries next to its older aerospace (Avco Corporation), transportation equipment (truck body and trailer manufacturing), and fabricated metals manufactures.

Like many subregional nodal centers of its size, Nashville remains a strong distribution point for its hinterland. The strength of its transportation and communication sector is shared between communication (Southern Central Bell Telephone employs 4,500) and trucking (which employed close to 8,000 people in 1976). Nashville, however, lacks the special strength in air transportation and utilities that are found in Charlotte.

CHARLOTTE

The overall image projected by the Charlotte SMSA is that of an economy acting as a strong subregional nodal center combined with a solid manufacturing base (primarily textile).

As a subregional nodal center, the growth of Charlotte seems to have largely benefited from the rapid growth of its hinter-land—the Piedmont region of the Carolinas. First and foremost, Charlotte stands out as an exceptionally strong center of distribution, located at the crossroads of some of the key highways of the southeastern region. Both its trucking and wholesaling industries are very dynamic. The rise of employment in trucking is due in part to the presence of several large and rapidly growing trucking companies (Johnson Motor Lines, UPS, Thurston Motor Lines) and is sparked by demand for the distribution of chemicals and petroleum products, electrical goods and hardware supplies, motor vehicles, and textiles. In dollar volume of wholesale trade, the Charlotte SMSA ranks 22nd in the nation, which is remarkable in the light of the fact that it is only the 66th-largest population center!

Charlotte has also emerged as a center of operation for utilities companies. Duke Power employs more than 5,000 people in the SMSA, including a large construction, engineering, and professional staff, and Southern Bell, more than 2,500 people. Charlotte has also become a major airport center for the region (Eastern Airlines employs over 1,000 people), handling a volume of traffic that is unusual for an SMSA of its size (Noyelle and Stanback, forthcoming).

Charlotte has also experienced a relatively strong development of its complex of corporate activities. The SMSA is a headquarters center for a number of large textile firms (Cannon Mills of the Fortune 500, Textiles Inc. of the second Fortune 500) as well as smaller regional and local textile and synthetic fibers companies (Celanese-Fibers Industries has made Charlotte its "other" headquarters city, next to New York) and is a preferred site for the head offices of the divisions of large firms engaged in dyeing and textile processing. In all it is the seat for more than 34 divisions of 24 of the Fortune 500, an unusually high number for an SMSA of its size (Noyelle and Stanback, forthcoming).

But even more than through its headquarters and divisional head offices, Charlotte stands out as a banking center. North Carolina has a well-developed branch banking system, and Charlotte is home base of NCNB (26th-largest bank in the nation) and First Union National Bank of North Carolina (55th-largest bank in the nation). Also important is a major facility of the other leading North Carolina bank, Wachovia (a Winston-Salem-based banking concern and another of the top 50 U.S. commercial banks). This strong banking presence is partly related to the fact that a major check-clearing facility of the Federal Reserve Bank is located in Charlotte, and more importantly to the fact that Charlotte has capitalized on the banking needs of the Piedmont counties of the Carolinas. Charlotte is also active in the insurance business, with All State Insurance, a subsidiary of Sears, Roebuck, employing more than 750 employees, and Equitable Life Insurance maintaining its southeastern regional office in the city.

The manufacturing sector of the SMSA is largely textile (primarily located in Gaston County), although textile production has declined in terms of relative importance over the years. The structure of the sector is that of an industry split (in employment terms) fairly evenly between the large textile corporations (e.g. Cone Mills, Burlington Industries, J. P. Stevens, Cannon Mills, American & Efird) on one hand, and regional and local companies, many of which are substantial firms (e.g., Belmont Heritage, A. M. Smyrre Mfg.), on the other.

In addition, Charlotte has a small employment base in the manufacture of guided missile components and their assembly (linked to Douglas Aircraft) and in the manufacture of machinery, mostly for the textile industry. More recently, it has diversified into the chemical industry, partly to provide for some of the needs of the textile industry (fibers, dyes, and organic pigments).

Charlotte is relatively weak in its residentiary sectors (retail and mainly consumer services), in the government sector, and in health and education. Despite its role as a regional metropolis, Charlotte boasts neither a major university nor a teaching hospital.*

In sum, Charlotte appears to have developed around a fairly well balanced private sector of small, medium, and large-sized firms, with a certain degree of linkage within and among industries. Many of the large and very large firms in Charlotte are essentially firms that have grown in concert with the region. On the other hand, Charlotte has developed without the assistance of a burgeoning public or nonprofit sector.

Conclusion

To conclude, this chapter has shown that, beyond some of the similarities suggested by the simple typology presented in Chapter 2, the seven metropolitan places under study have been characterized by significantly different experiences of economic transformation.

Atlanta, Denver, Phoenix, and Columbus have been characterized by the development of agglomerations of corporate offices and producer services along with other key service activities (distributive services, government and nonprofit functions), although this development remains markedly weaker in the case of Phoenix. But while manufacturing remains an important source of employment in Columbus, the three other places, Atlanta, Denver, and Phoenix, are relatively heavily dependent on their retail and consumer service sectors.

Charlotte and Nashville have established themselves as strong centers of distribution, but both have also displayed some success in developing their complex of corporate activities. At the same time, however, Charlotte continues to be dependent on its textile industry, while Nashville is an important center of government and nonprofit activities.

Buffalo, on the other hand, has shown little capacity to move away from a long-standing dependency on manufacturing and

---

*Charlotte is the home of one of the more recently developed branches of the University of North Carolina, however, and it has succeeded in developing an excellent nonteaching medical center, which serves the metropolitan area.

seems unable to find new directions for rejuvenation of its economic base.

Thus, differences must be understood in terms of both the functional role each center serves in the overall hierarchy of urban places and each place's own, particular, developmental history. In the chapter that follows we seek to determine the impact of these differences on the behavior of the respective metropolitan labor markets.

CHAPTER 6

The Impact of the Transformation
on Earnings and Mobility

This chapter examines for the seven SMSAs two basic measures of labor market conditions: earnings distributions and job mobility. The measures, based on the Continuous Work History Sample (CWHS) materials, are somewhat crude but nevertheless revealing. They lead us to two general findings: (1) that the distribution of earnings varies among SMSAs, with some places characterized by a substantial number of medium-paid jobs and others by a sharper dichotomy between poorly paid and well-paid jobs; and (2) that overall metropolitan economic growth influences the willingness of workers to move about in the labor market in search of betterment of their positions, but that, regardless of growth, certain of the SMSAs are characterized by higher levels of job hopping than others as workers seek, apparently with relatively little success, jobs with higher levels of pay and more adequate protection.

Differences among Labor Markets in the Earnings of Various Worker Groups

Although the CWHS materials are made available in a form that does not provide information relating to earnings distribution by industry, it is possible to examine the average earnings of the various worker group cells (e.g. stayers, new entrants, job movers, and inmigrants by sex and race) with sixteen cells in each industry.* Average earnings of worker groups in each industry in each SMSA have been grouped within five earnings categories, making use of normalized earnings: 1.60 and more, 1.20 to 1.59, .80 to 1.19, .40 to .79, and .39 and less.†

The data presented must be analyzed with care since they do not represent a conventional distribution of workers among earnings brackets, but rather a distribution of the various groups of covered workers (e.g., white male stayer, white male new entrants, white male job movers, white male inmigrants, black male stayers, etc.) according to average earnings in each group. Admittedly, the averages cover up earnings distributions within groups. For example, we do not know the distribution of earnings among white male stayers in FIRE in Charlotte. Moreover, it is likely that there is a greater dispersion of earnings among individual workers in some groups than in others. White male stayers are likely to vary far more in earnings than white male new entrants or even white female stayers, since mature white males find employment across a much wider spectrum of occupations in terms of earnings than do new entrants or even mature white women. Finally, there is the additional difficulty that the worker group cells are not of the same size. For example, white male stayers account for, on average, 45 percent of employment in construction, but only 16 percent in other services.

Nevertheless, the procedure followed does permit a fairly

---

*Only two racial classifications, white and black, are employed. The cell sizes for the remaining class, *other*, are too small for analysis, except in Denver and Phoenix.

†These normalized earnings relate to average earnings of covered workers in each SMSA. Thus, 1.60 equals 160 percent of average earnings in a given SMSA. This makes comparisons among places easier by avoiding the problem of adjusting for regional differences in wage levels. This procedure tends to bias slightly the picture of earnings distribution among groups in places which have a concentration of either well-paid or poorly paid jobs by shifting the average of earnings of the total covered workforce toward the predominant group and causing extreme values to be relatively low or high. Thus, in Charlotte the highest earnings are expressed as a multiple of somewhat low average SMSA earnings influenced by its important, relatively low-wage textile industry, while in Buffalo they are expressed as multiples of relatively high SMSA average earnings, influenced by its high-wage manufacturing complex.

Table 6.1 Distribution of Covered Workforce among Earnings Classes, Based on Average Earnings of Worker Groups, Seven SMSAs, 1975 (in percentages)

Earnings classes[a]	Atlanta	Denver	Buffalo	Phoenix	Columbus	Nashville	Charlotte	Average[b]
1.60 and above	9.1	17.3	0.2	13.2	9.7	7.7	16.0	9.6
1.20–1.59	27.9	17.7	42.5	19.5	27.9	25.4	22.9	24.7
.80–1.19	19.8	22.6	24.5	29.9	20.2	28.2	21.8	23.5
.40–.79	36.7	36.0	24.5	31.9	35.3	34.0	35.1	34.5
less than .40	6.5	6.4	8.3	5.6	6.9	4.7	4.2	6.0

[a]Earnings classes are based on average 1975 SMSA earnings and expressed as relatives (1.00 equals average SMSA earnings).
[b]Modified averages, lowest and highest values dropped. Percentages do not add to 100.

Note: Employment in each sex-race category (white male, black male, white female, black female, other male, other female) in each of five worker groups (stayers, in-movers, outmovers, inmigrants, new entrants) in each industry classification is allocated to one of the earnings classes according to average earnings in the subclassification of workers. Average earnings are expressed as relatives, with average 1975 SMSA earnings for all covered workers equal to 1.00 (100 percent).

Source: U.S. Bureau of Economic Analysis, *Ten Percent Continuous Work History Sample.*

detailed breakdown in each industry category. Such analysis of distribution of employment of these subsets in terms of average earnings reveals distinctive differences both among different industries within SMSA and among SMSAs for like industries.

The average distribution of employment for the seven places (Table 6.1) reveals a strong tendency for the jobs to be more numerous in the lower than in the average earnings range, with bracket 4 (40 percent to 79 percent of average) — *not bracket 3 (80 to 119 percent)* — being by far the most heavily represented earnings category. Although there is considerable variation among SMSAs, this characteristic holds for all places except Buffalo, where the most populous category is bracket 2 (120 to 159 percent), reflecting the effect of its relatively large and unionized industrial sector and its relatively poorly developed services. Note also that the more concentrated distribution of employment in earnings brackets 2 and 3 in Nashville may suggest a better-balanced earnings structure than in the five remaining places.

The sources of variation in earnings distribution among places are difficult to analyze, since they arise from a combination of differences in the industrial composition of employment (i.e., the relative importance of various industries) and in the occupational and earnings structure of employment within industries. Table 6.2 is set up in such a way as to facilitate analysis. Part A indicates which industry groups are relatively large in terms of shares of SMSA employment and which are relatively small.* For example, TCU and FIRE are relatively small industrial categories everywhere, whereas wholesale-retail (largely retail) and other services are relatively large. Manufacturing is, as noted in Chapter 4, the category that varies most widely in terms of share of covered employment (it accounts for 38 percent of covered employment in Buffalo, only 16 percent in Phoenix). Nevertheless, it is, on average, a major employment category.

Part B presents a modified average (seven SMSAs) of the distribution of employment among earnings brackets in each industry group and for total employment, providing a standard against which distributions in individual SMSAs may be judged.

Part C provides a means of interpreting earnings distributions of employment by industry for each SMSA. In each SMSA, earnings cells (1,2,3, etc.) in which the percentage is significantly greater or less (in parentheses) than average are identified.† These cells are defined arbitrarily as those with shares of workers which differ by 2 percent or more from the comparable average percentage shown in Part B, and are underlined where the cells differ by 10 percentage points or more. For example, in manufacturing Columbus is found to have higher-than-average employment in the 1.20-1.59 bracket (i.e. 2 to 10 percentage points larger than the average of 47.6 percent), much higher than

---

*The information presented in Part A of this table is based on the 10 percent sample of the CWHS, which includes only workers covered by the Social Security system. Accordingly, it is not comparable to the data presented earlier in Chapter 5.

†The reader will find percentages for each worker group in each industry in Appendix Table 4.

average employment in the .80 to 1.19 bracket (10 percentage points or more larger than the average of 22.2 percent), and much less than average employment in the .40 to .79 bracket (at least 10 percentage points less than the average of 23.7 percent). Manufacturing employment in Columbus in brackets one and five (1.60 and above, and less than .40) does not differ significantly from the average of zero shown in Part B, and these earnings brackets are not identified in Part C.

In spite of the limitations of the earnings distribution measure and the coarseness of the industrial classifications, the analysis in Table 6.2 reveals significant similarities as well as certain differences among SMSAs. Similarities among distributions are the greatest for the service industries. In the case of TCU, despite some variations in the distribution of earnings among SMSAs (Part C), in no instance are the favorable earnings tendencies of this industry group lost. These industries tend to offer well-paid jobs regardless of sex and race in all SMSAs, undoubtedly because these industries are dominated by large firms with relatively favorable ladders of mobility. On the average, more than 70 percent of the jobs offered by these industries fall in the top two income brackets (Part B). It seems likely that in those places where we find the largest shares of TCU employment in the top income bracket (Atlanta, Phoenix, Columbus, and Charlotte), these industries offer the highest wage levels in the economy.

The most general characteristic of the wholesale-retail (mostly retail) sector is the predominance of low-paid jobs (because of retail) — almost 60 percent of employment on average in the less than .80 earnings brackets. Here we see clearly how the residentiary-type services tend to weigh service-oriented metropolitan economies toward low-income employment. Atlanta, Charlotte, and Buffalo depart slightly from the average pattern, but the basic characteristic of disproportionately low earnings still remains.

The two places with a strong wholesale sector, Charlotte and Atlanta, exhibit a larger proportion of wage earners in the 1.20 and above earnings ranges. Charlotte's small percentage of workers in the low earnings category stems not only from its larger-than-average proportion of wholesale employment but also from its lack of a strong retail sector. In Buffalo the share of

Table 6.2 Selected Data Relating to Distribution of Covered Workforce among Industries and among Earnings Classes (by industry), Seven SMSAs, 1975

A: Distribution (%) among industries

	Total	Construction	Manufacturing	TCU	Wholesale/ Retail	FIRE	Other services
Atlanta	100.0	7.6	20.4	7.3	28.1	9.5	27.2
Denver	100.0	8.5	18.1	8.1	32.2	8.9	24.3
Buffalo	100.0	3.8	37.7	5.5	23.1	4.8	25.1
Phoenix	100.0	7.8	15.8	6.1	30.1	7.4	32.7
Columbus	100.0	5.6	26.0	5.9	29.0	9.4	24.2
Nashville	100.0	7.3	27.7	4.9	25.6	6.6	27.8
Charlotte	100.0	9.0	29.6	10.0	25.9	5.4	20.2
Average, 7 SMSA[a]	–	7.4	26.0	6.6	27.7	7.5	25.7

B: Average distribution (%) among earnings classes 7 SMSAs[a,b]

	Total	Construction	Manufacturing	TCU	Wholesale/ Retail	FIRE	Other services
Class 1: 1.60 and above	9.6	–	–	45.0	–	21.6	15.7
Class 2: 1.20–1.59	24.7	53.5	47.6	26.6	25.7	10.0	3.1
Class 3: .80–1.19	23.5	27.9	22.2	19.7	12.9	35.3	33.3
Class 4: .40–.79	34.5	20.0	23.7	10.3	40.1	32.8	43.9
Class 5: Less than .40	6.0	2.3	–	–	17.3	–	1.7

C: Earnings classes
with above average employment[c]

Atlanta	2,(3),4	(2),3,<u>4</u>	<u>2</u>,(3),4	1,(3),(4)	<u>2</u>,(3),(5)	2,(3),4	(1),2,(3),4,5
Denver	1,(2),4	2,3,(<u>4</u>)	1,(2),3,(4)	(<u>2</u>),<u>3</u>,(4)	3	(2),3	1,(2),(<u>3</u>),(<u>4</u>)
Buffalo	(<u>1</u>),2,(<u>4</u>)	<u>2</u>,(3)	<u>2</u>,3,(<u>4</u>)	(<u>1</u>),2,3,4	(3),(4),<u>5</u>	(<u>1</u>),<u>2</u>,(<u>3</u>),<u>4</u>	(<u>1</u>),<u>2</u>,3,(4)
Phoenix	1,(2),3,(4)	<u>2</u>,<u>4</u>,(5)	<u>1</u>,(2),3,(4)	1,(2),<u>3</u>	3	4	1,(2),3,(4)
Columbus	2,(3)	<u>2</u>,(3),4	2,3,(4)	1,(3),4	4,5	1,(2),3,(4)	1,(2),(<u>3</u>),<u>4</u>,5
Nashville	3	(2),3,<u>4</u>	(2),(<u>3</u>),<u>4</u>	(1),2,(3),4	3	3,(4)	<u>3</u>,(<u>4</u>),(5)
Charlotte	1,(3)	(2),<u>3</u>,4	(2),(<u>3</u>),<u>4</u>	1,2,(3),(4)	<u>1</u>,(<u>2</u>),(3),(4),(5)	1,(3)	2,<u>3</u>,(<u>4</u>),(5)

[a] Modified averages, lowest and highest value dropped.

[b] See Table 6.1 for description of method of distributing workers among earnings classes in each SMSA.

[c] Part C indicates those earnings classes in which the percentage of employment is significantly greater (or significantly less) than the average shown in part B. Percentages are considered to be significantly greater or less (in parentheses) than average if they differ by 2 percentage points or more. Where variations are 10 percentage points or more, the earnings class is underlined. Detail is shown in Appendix Table 4.

Source: U.S. Bureau of Economic Analysis, *Ten Percent Continuous Work History Sample.*

wholesale-retail employment in the less than .40 earnings bracket is especially large. This probably reflects in part a high level of competition among women and male new entrants for low-end retail jobs under conditions of high levels of general unemployment.*

FIRE demonstrates the kind of polarization of earnings that was found earlier for this industrial category in the nation's labor force. The 22 percent (average) of the workforce in FIRE within the 1.60 and above earnings bracket indicates the existence of a substantial number of well-paid jobs (see Part B), but only 10 percent are classified within the 1.20 and 1.59 bracket. Further down the spectrum, 35 percent of workers fall in the .80 to 1.19 average earnings range, and an almost equal number in the .40 to .79 bracket. Although there are variations (Part C), all SMSAs except Buffalo approximate this pattern of distribution. The distinctly different nature of Buffalo's economy is again apparent. What is especially interesting is the very large proportion of FIRE employment (62 percent—see Appendix Table 4) in earnings bracket 4, indicating, as in wholesale-retail, a heavy competition for low-end service jobs in a failing manufacturing-oriented economy.

Data for the other services category are difficult to analyze because of the heterogeneous composition of this industrial grouping. The principal observation is that these services add to the tendency of service-oriented metropolitan economies to show a bimodal earnings distribution. On average (Part B), 16 percent of employment (largely male stayers) fall in the 1.60 earnings bracket, virtually none in the 1.20 to 1.59 bracket, roughly one-third in the .80 to 1.19 range, and about 45 percent in the less than .79 brackets. Nashville, Charlotte, and Buffalo appear to fare best, with much larger than average shares of employment in either bracket 2 or bracket 3. In Nashville, this may be the case because of its well-developed nonprofit services, in Charlotte because of the relatively small role played by the poorly paid, mainly consumer service sector in its economy; but Buffalo seems

---

*This probably reflects, also, the sharp difference between low-paid retail jobs and other kinds of employment in an economy otherwise characterized by relatively well-paid jobs for those who manage to find employment.

more difficult to explain. Similarly, for reasons that are not clear, Atlanta has the largest percentage of other services employment in bracket 5 (see Appendix Table 4).

Our conclusion based on Table 6.2 is that each of the four service categories tends to retain its characteristic pattern of distribution of employment among earning brackets in most of the SMSAs studied. There are differences among places and these deserve more detailed study, but they do not appear to be as important as the characteristic differences among industry groups.

In manufacturing and construction, however, there are sharper variations among SMSAs. In general there seem to be two different patterns of earnings in the manufacturing sector. Places well endowed with an old, heavy manufacturing sector that relies primarily on a skilled and well-unionized workforce will tend to provide for sizable numbers of medium-range and relatively well paid jobs. This is clearly the case in both Columbus and Buffalo. All other places exhibit as more dichotomized pattern of earnings distribution among worker groups in manufacturing. The phenomenon is very clear in Atlanta, Denver, and Phoenix and even more so in Nashville and Charlotte, which are characterized by an overconcentration of workers in bracket 4. With better data in hand, we could probably argue that this dichotomy reflects the disparities that exist in the manufacturing base of these SMSAs, on the one hand *between relatively high paying and relatively low paying industries* (for instance, in Phoenix between the aerospace sector and some low paying manufacturing industries, such as food or printing) and, on the other hand, *within high-technology industries* between pools of highly skilled employees (engineers, technicians, or supervisors) and pools of relatively low-wage, low-skilled production workers (again in Phoenix in the semiconductor industry, between usually male engineers and technicians and usually female or minority assemblers).

Finally, in construction patterns differ largely in terms of the relative importance of brackets 2, 3, and 4. In Denver, Buffalo, Phoenix, and Columbus, construction workers are relatively well paid, with the shares of employment in bracket 2 (1.2 to 1.59) at least 10 percentage points greater than average. Brackets 3 and/or 4 are correspondingly less. In the southeastern SMSAs (Atlanta, Nashville, and Charlotte), however, they are less well paid: the shares of employment in bracket 2 are at least 10 percentage points lower than average, with brackets 3 and/or 4 correspondingly greater.

Variations in Worker Mobility Patterns

STAYERS

In Chapter 4 we observed that differences among industry groups in average ratios of stayers to total employment at the beginning of the period were indicative of basic differences in labor market conditions, primarily in growth and in quality of the employment provided, as measured by opportunities for the upgrading of the individual worker's status in the labor force. Undoubtedly, age composition of the work force also plays a role in the behavior of these ratios, although it was not possible to adjust here for such influence.

We now return to these measures. Table 6.3 presents, separately for males and females, the percentage of stayers to the initial covered workforce in each industry group in each SMSA, along with averages of percentages across industries for each place and across places for each industry.

A major observation is that the average percentage of stayers varies significantly between sexes, among industries, and among SMSAs.

Regarding the industry averages, we note the following:

1. Manufacturing appears to offer relatively favorable protection and attractive employment for both men and women, although average ratios are typically somewhat higher for males.

2. In TCU, average percentages are high for both male and female, apparently because of opportunities for relatively high wages and internal upward job mobility, as noted earlier.

3. In the FIRE industries, which we have observed to be segmented in terms of earnings, with a small layer of high-status professional or managerial jobs and a much larger one of lower status, essentially dead-end, clerical-type jobs, the percentage of male stayers is typically somewhat above that found in wholesale-retail, but below manufacturing and TCU. The level for males

Table 6.3 Stayers as a Percentage of Initial Covered Workforce by Industry and by SMSA; 1971-1973; Averages for Seven SMSAs, 1971-1973 and 1973-1975

	Atlanta	Denver	Buffalo	Phoenix	Columbus	Nashville	Charlotte	Average[b] 1971-1973	Average[b] 1973-1975
All males									
All industries	50.4 (7)	52.7 (5)	66.6 (6)	50.8 (6)	57.5 (3)	60.6 (2)	56.5 (4)	55.6	48.9
Construction	41.4 (7)	54.1 (3)	63.0 (1)	45.2 (6)	54.5 (2)	47.8 (4)	46.8 (5)	49.7	43.0
Manufacturing	55.2 (5)	54.4 (6)	71.7 (1)	48.9 (7)	60.4 (3)	67.2 (2)	59.8 (4)	59.4	53.7
TCU	62.2 (6)	62.1 (7)	74.5 (1)	66.7 (5)	73.2 (2)	69.0 (4)	69.6 (3)	68.1	61.9
Wholesale/Retail	48.9 (6)	50.1 (5)	53.2 (3)	45.4 (7)	51.4 (4)	54.8 (1)	54.0 (2)	51.5	45.0
FIRE	55.7 (3)	53.4 (5)	64.3 (1)	50.4 (6)	59.8 (2)	55.4 (4)	48.1 (7)	55.0	48.1
Other services	48.7 (6)	47.0 (7)	59.7 (1)	52.1 (5)	52.7 (3)	59.2 (2)	51.8 (4)	53.0	49.0
All females[a]									
All industries	47.3 (7)	49.0 (6)	59.7 (2)	49.7 (5)	54.0 (4)	61.0 (1)	56.2 (3)	53.7	48.8
Manufacturing	55.0 (5)	49.7 (6)	62.9 (2)	39.1 (7)	58.1 (4)	64.1 (1)	62.5 (3)	57.6	48.2
TCU	31.9 (7)	56.8 (6)	68.4 (1)	66.0 (4)	67.3 (3)	67.6 (2)	65.5 (5)	64.6	67.0
Wholesale/Retail	44.5 (6)	44.9 (5)	49.7 (3)	39.9 (7)	49.3 (4)	50.2 (2)	50.6 (1)	47.7	40.7
FIRE	52.3 (3)	49.7 (5)	59.6 (1)	45.9 (7)	58.2 (2)	51.8 (4)	46.3 (6)	51.7	50.3
Other services	55.1 (5)	49.5 (7)	63.0 (2)	55.5 (4)	52.1 (6)	65.1 (1)	58.4 (3)	56.8	54.9

[a]Female employment in construction is relatively unimportant and this category is omitted.
[b]Modified averages. Highest and lowest values are dropped.

Note: Numbers in parentheses are rankings among SMSAs.

Source: U.S. Bureau of Economic Analysis, *Ten Percent Continuous Work History Sample.*

relative to that of other services varies sharply—being higher in four places, lower in three. The average percentage is lower for females, ranking fourth among the five industry groups in most places.

4. In the wholesale-retail classification where the dominant in-dustry, retailing, tends to offer mostly dead-end, low-status, low-paid jobs, managerial and staff positions do not provide sufficient opportunity for improvement to induce a large number of workers to remain employed. The percentage of stayers is smallest in this classification for both males and females.

5. The heterogeneous other services classification appears to offer attractive opportunities for a larger share of women than men (i.e., the percentage of stayers is higher for female than male workers). For males, other services ranks fourth in 1971–73 and third in 1973–75. For females it ranks third in 1971–73 and sec-ond in 1973–75.

When we examine the percentages on an SMSA-by-SMSA basis, the most striking finding is that there is a marked tendency for certain places to show relatively high percentages across in-dustries, others relatively low, but for the relative standings among industries to be similar in each SMSA. Table 6.3 presents rankings of SMSAs based on comparisons of percentages within each industry group. The ranks of individual SMSAs are not identical among industries but show well-developed tendencies in most instances (especially for males) to conform in a general way to the following sequence: 1st (highest) Buffalo, 2nd Nashville, 3rd Columbus, 4th Charlotte, 5th Denver, 6th Phoenix, and 7th (lowest) Atlanta. The sequences for males and for females are slightly different.

What explanations can be offered for this tendency for certain SMSAs to have relatively high ratios in all or most industries, and for others relatively low ratios? In Chapter 4 it was suggested that the tendency of workers to remain in existing jobs may be related to rate of overall employment growth. When growth is rapid, workers may perceive that job opportunities are opening up across a broad front and that risks involved in changing employ-ment in a new industry are minimal. When growth is slow, the opposite perception would seem likely.

A comparison of overall growth rates (based on all industries, all sex and race growth rates between 1971 and 1973) and average percentage of stayers 1971–1973 suggests that growth is an important but by no means exclusive influence. When SMSAs are ranked in order of growth and inversely in terms of average percentage of stayers (lowest percentage ranks first, etc.), the following relationships are noted:

	Growth: rank	Stayer percentages: inverse rank
Phoenix	1 (highest)	2
Denver	2	3
Nashville	3	6
Charlotte	4	4
Columbus	5	5
Atlanta	6	1 (lowest)
Buffalo	7 (lowest)	7 (highest)

Thus, Atlanta's and Nashville's sharp departure from the general rank-order relationship raises the question of whether or not factors other than growth influence the overall level of stayers. In the case of Atlanta, it may well be that lagged growth effects are being observed. Atlanta, it has already been noted, experienced rates of overall employment growth similar to those of Phoenix and Denver for the more extended periods, 1959–1969 and 1969–1976. It is not unlikely that worker expectations were influenced by these longer-run conditions during the years 1971–1973. But Atlanta's industrial-occupational structure is also very likely a contributing factor. As we observed earlier, Atlanta's transformation to the services has been characterized by a strong tendency to create large numbers of low-paid, low-status, dead-end jobs (either clerical jobs in the corporate complex or service-worker jobs in retail and mainly consumer services). These are typically jobs characterized by high levels of turnover (i.e., low levels of stayers).

Nashville, on the other hand, seems to represent the opposite situation. Although it experienced relatively favorable growth rates, its average percentage of stayers was high for both males and females. This seems consistent with our earlier findings that Nashville's overall earnings distribution is the least dichotomized and that its other services sector, which is larger than average, appears to have a relatively favorable earnings distribution. Taken as a whole these observations seem to indicate that Nashville's workers find relatively less pressure to move from job to job in search of what they regard as more favorable arrangements.

To conclude, we must not overemphasize the role of growth. The quality of the labor market is no less important as a structural element of the transformation. While high growth ameliorates labor market conditions, a high proportion of industries with low-end service jobs tends to establish limitations on achievements for most workers. It is in this light that we must seek to understand the problems — current and potential — of urban economies. Metropolitan areas which offer considerable opportunities for worker achievement under conditions of growth are likely to face difficult problems as they mature and begin to stabilize, if they are strongly oriented to those services that offer a dearth of opportunities for upward mobility.

JOB MOVERS

The previous section has focused on stayers, a group of workers in each industry who are likely to hold the most satisfactory jobs. But during every period, vacancies are created by departures from the workforce, by outmigration and, at the industry level, by job outmovers who are changing industry of employment either voluntarily (to seek better situations) or involuntarily (because they have been discharged). At the same time, job vacancies in particular industries are being filled by new entrants, inmigrants, and job inmovers (job outmovers from other industries).

The processes of worker entry and change are complex, and a thorough analysis accounting for all flows would require a statistical investigation involving examination of a much larger number of places than is being studied here. We concentrate on job movers because their behavior sheds light on the actions workers take as they search for higher pay and improved working conditions.

Table 6.4 indicates that the total flows of job movers are quite large — 10 percent or higher for males over a two-year period in the majority of SMSAs. These magnitudes are all the more

Table 6.4   Total 1973–1975 Flows of Job Out-Movers as a Percentage of the 1973 Initial Covered Workforce, Male and Female

	All males	All females
Atlanta	10.6	12.1
Denver	11.4	10.0
Buffalo	6.8	7.5
Phoenix	13.9	9.5
Columbus	7.9	7.6
Nashville	10.4	8.4
Charlotte	10.6	8.7

Note: In each SMSA, the number of all male (or female) out-movers is equal to the number of all male (or female) in-movers.

Source: U.S. Bureau of Economic Analysis, *Ten Percent Continuous Work History Sample.*

noteworthy in light of the fact that they account for only part of job hopping; intraindustry, firm-to-firm job movement is not recorded in the available CWHS data.

The measures of job movers like those of stayers may be expected to reflect the influence of demographic structure, growth, and quality of the labor market specific to each place. Under given conditions of demographic structure and growth, we expect to find workers attempting to move from the worst to the best industries, with the probability of their effecting such a move being influenced by the overall existence (or lack thereof) of upward-mobility ladders in the industries of their present employment. Where such upward mobility is lacking the worker tends to move more frequently. Table 6.5 indicates that the behavior of the job movers is essentially consistent with that which was found for the job stayers. Except for the two anomalies of Columbus and Nashville females, the correlation between the rankings of the ratios of job staying and the ratios of job outmovers is very high.

Table 6.5 Comparison of the Rankings of the Ratios of Job Stayers and Job Out-Movers to Initial Covered Workforce, All Industries, 1971–1973

	Rankings (male)		Rankings (female)	
	Ratios of job stayers[a]	Ratios of job out-movers[b]	Ratios of job stayers[a]	Ratios of job out-movers[b]
Atlanta	7	5	7	7
Denver	5	6	6	6
Buffalo	1	1	2	1
Phoenix	6	7	5	5
Columbus	3	2	4	2
Nashville	2	3	1	4
Charlotte	4	4	3	3

[a]Highest ratio of job stayers to initial covered workforce ranked first.
[b]Lowest ratio of job out-movers to initial covered workforce ranked first.

Source: U.S. Bureau of Economic Analysis, *Ten Percent Continuous Work History Sample.*

Conclusion

Several concluding observations seem warranted. In the most general way, this study of the impact of the transformation on earnings and mobility in the seven metropolitan labor markets confirms and clarifies some of the trends noted in Chapters 2 and 3. First it confirms that the service transformation described in Chapter 2 has had a rather dramatic impact on the labor market of the seven metropolitan places with, however, some degree of differentiation among places. Second, it suggests that, not unlike what was found for the nation as a whole (Chapter 3), this economic transformation of metropolitan markets has translated into a tendency toward bifurcated structures of earnings and job attributes for workers—again, with some noticeable differences among places.

Buffalo, with its overall earnings structure indicative of an economy relatively well layered with "medium" wage jobs, appears to be representative of a structure prevalent in the past. Indeed, the great difficulties encountered by Buffalo in maintaining its economic standing is indicative of a structure that, for a multitude of reasons, appears increasingly more obsolete in light of the directions taken by the current transformation.

These new directions are indicated by the developments that have taken place in the six other SMSAs. Our analysis indicates an increasing divergence within metropolitan economies between "good" and "bad" jobs evidenced by a polarization of the earnings structure and an apparent lack of upward mobility ladders, observed most readily through the relative dearth of "middle-layer" jobs. While this trend is most easily associated with the rise of service (as opposed to nonservice) employment, it appears to underline the transformation of the manufacturing sector as well. The increased separation between production and administrative functions (witnessed by the increased spatial separation between production and administrative establishments) and the increased division of the work process within both production and corporate administration (resulting in a greater polarization between skilled and nonskilled workers) seem clearly in evidence in the places studied.

The recent development in Columbus indicates that metropolitan economies within the old industrial belt are not alien to this transformation. The example of Nashville seems to suggest that an economy may experience a more acceptable transformation process where it is possible to foster the development of those services industries which tend to pay good wages and create at least limited opportunities for improvement in the workers' job status.

These observations raise major issues, both at the national and the metropolitan level, which deserve substantial attention. They are treated in the next and concluding chapter.

CHAPTER 7

The Problems of Work
in a Service Economy

This study of seven metropolitan labor markets in transition has sought to make some key observations regarding the kinds of special problems and opportunities that are being generated by two fundamental and closely related changes at play in the economy: the rise of the service industries and the shift to white collar work. This final chapter summarizes the main findings, develops some major issues, and concludes with selected policy recommendations.

Summary of Findings

Following a short introductory chapter (1), Chapter 2 opens the analysis with a general statement to the effect that the U.S. economy is undergoing a major structural transformation characterized by a change in the nature of the goods and services it produces (a change in *what* we produce) and a change in the way it organizes production and work (a change in *how* we produce). A six-class typology grouping of the service industries into distributive, producer, retailing, mainly consumer, nonprofit, and government services is suggested to facilitate analysis of some of the processes at work. Three major factors are then identified as being at the core of the transformation process: the increasing size of the market, the rise of the large corporation, and the rising importance of government and nonprofit institutions in the economy.

Next we argue that this major transformation of the economy has been accompanied by a transformation of both the economic base of individual cities and the overall structure of the urban system. For purpose of exposition, the system of cities is divided into three population size tiers, comprising large, medium, and small metropolitan areas (36, 104, and 126 places, respectively). A simple typology of places based on specialization of metropolitan economies is then introduced to distinguish among different types of service-oriented and goods production-oriented centers. An examination of the recent transformation of the urban hierarchy indicates that, among large and medium-sized places, many centers, which were once heavily engaged in manufacturing are now largely service-oriented. The most prominent type emerging among these new service economies is that of the *nodal* place, whose primary functions are to ensure the distribution of goods within its general market area and to provide producer and headquarters services to private sector firms. In terms of the above six-way classification of services, nodal places are characterized by their unusual strength in the distributive and producer services. Nodal places also tend to be characterized by a relatively large nonprofit and government (federal and state) sector which, in large part, caters to the needs of private sector firms active in the locale and its surrounding markets. Finally, we are careful to stress that size remains an important determinant of structure, with regional and subregional nodal places for example, differing in terms of market areas served and the range and level of corporate services provided. As regards the seven SMSAs selected for this study, Atlanta, Denver, Phoenix, and Columbus are identified as *regional nodal* centers, Nashville and Charlotte as *subregional nodal* centers, and Buffalo as a declining *production* (manufacturing) center.

In Chapter 3, our attention is directed to an analysis of the impact of the shift to services and the rise of white collar forms of work on the nation's labor force.

While strongly associated with the rising importance of service industries, the shift to white collar work has occurred within both nonservice and service industries. In both cases, this shift has been brought about in large measure by the rise of centralized administrative and planning functions within large corporations and by technological changes at the level of production or service delivery establishments, and has resulted in an increasing demand for managers, professionals, technicians, and clerical employees. But in terms of its overall impact on the nation's labor force, the most important shift is that resulting from the rise of employment in service industries and the relative employment stagnation of nonservice activities.

The study of the occupational structure of individual industries at the national level demonstrates that striking differences exist among industries in terms of occupational and jobs composition. Among the service industries in particular, distributive and government services tend to be relatively well paying industries, characterized by large numbers of "medium" and "good" jobs and by tendencies to develop internal labor markets offering the entering worker opportunities for occupational promotion and substantial earnings gains over the course of his or her tenure in the industry. Producer and nonprofit services are characterized by a sharper dichotomy between relatively very well paid and well-protected managers, professionals, and technicians, and relatively low-paid and less protected clerical and service workers, with generally poor opportunities for upward mobility for those in the lower echelons of employment. Finally, retail and mainly consumer services are typically poorly paying industries characterized by a plethora of low-ranking occupations and a dearth of "medium" or "good" job opportunities.

In Chapter 4, a preliminary analysis of the seven metropolitan labor markets based upon the *Ten-Percent Continuous Work History Sample* indicates that a number of the industry characteristics observed for the nation as a whole apply to the local level.

Not surprisingly, problems are found to be more serious for minority workers of either sex and for white females, who face major difficulties in moving up from largely dead-end, low paying occupations. For white females, this finding may be regarded as ironic in light of the dramatic increase in their participation in the labor force, since their expanded employment has provided a major contribution to the growth of service industries. Yet even among white female stayers, earnings reach only 90 percent of the all-worker average for the SMSAs studied and 50 percent of the average of white male stayers.

But the state of affairs is even worse among the other minority workers. Extremely serious is the situation among black male workers, who appear to have remained largely marginal to the development of the service industries in an era during which employment in the nonservice industries (where they have found somewhat better job opportunities) has been declining steadily.

In short, opportunities for upward mobility appear not only to be shrinking with growth in the service economy but to be largely restricted to white male workers. Furthermore, limited evidence relating to the experience of white male workers in the retail and mainly consumer industries indicates that those workers may also be facing restricted opportunities for improvement, at least as compared to their peers in other industries.

These industry-specific characteristics of employment suggest that among SMSAs differing mixes in industrial bases may lead to overall differences in labor market conditions.

The next two chapters address this possibility. Chapter 5 takes a more careful look at the economic structure of the seven SMSAs and their recent transformation. Several factors are suggested as likely to introduce differences in the developmental history of each place: overall growth conditions, industry mix, institutional structure of specific industry groups (large firms versus small firms, degree of unionization, etc.), and economic mission of establishments within industry groups (administrative versus production functions, etc.). Substantial differences among places indicate that a closer analysis of labor market conditions in each place is warranted. In Chapter 6 we return to an analysis of the data provided by the *Ten Percent Continuous Work History Sample* used earlier.

Chapters 5 and 6 reveal two major trends. First, while there is evidence of a transformation toward newer, more dichotomized employment systems in most of the SMSAs studied, it appears that the specific working balance among the historical and structural factors cited above can significantly retard, advance, or alter the process. Places in the more recently favored sunbelt regions appear more advanced in their transformation, although Columbus seems to indicate that selected places in the older industrial areas might not be far behind. Buffalo, on the other hand, demonstrates that older employment systems can still place a heavy stamp upon the labor market conditions of metropolitan areas that experienced their major development in an earlier era. Second, while the moving about of workers in a local labor market is typically associated with rapid growth that opens up new work opportunities, the trend toward high levels of jobhopping in the most service-oriented places appears to reflect also a basic inability on the part of large numbers of workers to find in these economies jobs with opportunities for upward mobility. These and other findings revealed by this study are taken up more carefully in the paragraphs that follow.

Truncated Patterns of Upward Mobility

The first order of problems arising from the transformations at work is largely nonspatial. It relates to the nature and quality of *work*, which come as a result of the occupational and earning structures that have developed in the service industries, in particular, and white collar employment systems, generally.

Through the course of their history, manufacturing and some of the service industries that developed earlier (e.g., TCU, wholesale, etc.) have tended to create employment systems that provide some opportunities for upward mobility tied to favorable expectations of long-term employment stability, and guaranteed earnings gains over the course of the individual's working life. Of course, conditions have varied across industries and among firms within industries. Large manufacturing firms have traditionally been better at providing acceptable employment conditions than their smaller counterparts, and certain industries have offered better pay conditions, job guarantees, and job ladders than others. In addition, trade unions have been instrumental in these developments. A major feature of employment systems in these industries has been a laddering of jobs, frequently *internal* to the firm or the industry, whereby, upon their entry into the labor force, workers are likely to find available the opportunity for some degree of occupational mobility, with the employer bearing the costs of the training necessary to their requalification (Doeringer and Piore, 1971; Freedman, 1976).

Yet while these general characteristics of work in the manufacturing sector and in selected service industries have, broadly speaking, obtained until recently, there is evidence that we may be witnessing the emergence of tendencies running counter to those just described. On the one hand, the rising importance of corporate service functions (management, sales, engineering, R&D) is bringing about the growth of office-based employment structures within the large manufacturing corporation, structures which resemble those found in some of the service industries (with large pools of clericals and lesser numbers of managers and professionals) (Chapters 2 and 3). On the other hand, the pressure of international competition is forcing large manufacturers to pay much greater attention to labor costs considerations, which often translates into an increased automation of production and a sharper bifurcation of the plant labor force between well-paid managers, engineers, and technicians and low-wage, low-skill assembly workers. This clearly seems the case in a number of high technology industries (e.g., semiconductor and consumer electronics), even though large corporations tend to dominate (e.g., Motorola, Honeywell, Texas Instruments) (see Chapters 5 and 6 for a discussion of manufacturing trends in several of the SMSAs examined).

By comparison with older industries, the services that have grown the most rapidly in the recent period have failed to offer built-in job ladders. Most service firms tend to be structured in such a way that the two poles of their occupational structure are dependent upon one another to ensure the existence and functioning of the firm, yet are poorly linked internally in a labor market sense. This problem is not unrelated to the issue of size of firms in the service industries although, as we argue in Chapters 2 and 3 (see Table 3.8), associating small firm size with services is an unwarranted simplification, as the picture differs substantially across service industries.

In the light of this increased polarization of labor markets and the decreasing importance of internal ladders, workers have had to seek new ways of achieving upgrading. These have come primarily through education and repeated change of employer (jobhopping).* Both are flawed with serious limitations.

Education is one avenue by which workers starting at the bottom of the occupational structure may hope to make the quantum leap needed to reach the upper strata. A major difficulty with the educational route (college or university) as it exists currently, however, is that such a model for career upgrading is probably a reasonable one only for the younger segments of the labor force. It requires an emotional and financial investment that the older worker, with greater commitments to his or her family, may rarely be able to afford. In addition, although educational opportunities may have become more equal among younger white workers, they remain relatively closed to minorities, if only because of inadequate primary and secondary schooling.

The other avenue for career upgrading, jobhopping, seems to rest on the assumption that through repeated changes of employers the individual worker will gain additional work experience, improve earnings, and ameliorate his or her occupational status in incremental ways. If, as appears to be the case, larger firms have become more restricted in the opportunities they offer for upgrading (Chapter 3), then it is the more dynamic among the small or medium-size firms that may open the best route for improvement, in that they provide for a work environment in which occupational positions are less strictly defined and in which being at the right place at the right time in lieu of more formal training or qualifications may mean a substantial improvement in one's position or responsibilities.

This avenue is likely to be a poor second best, however. In addition to structural limitations associated with the size of small firms (viability of the firm and truncated occupational ladders — see Chapter 3), women and minority workers still seem largely unable to break away from traditional job labeling in these firms. What they may expect to achieve through jobhopping is, at best, to enter an industry or a firm that offers a better pay scale and better guarantees of employment stability. As regards white male workers, for whom this avenue might be more promising

---

*In a spatial context, this may occur either through a change of employer within the same metropolitan labor market or by migrating to another urban area.

than for female or minority workers, opportunities hinge dangerously on the availability of promising openings in the right kind of small or medium-size firm. In this respect, our study of individual metropolitan markets seems to suggest that the size-hierarchy of firms varies enormously among places and that not all places are endowed equally. Several factors work to explain the presence or absence of such a network of firms, including the business history of the locale and the degree to which large firms present in the area have developed strong linkages with the local economy (thereby contributing to the maintenance and/or development of a network of smaller firms).

To conclude, while we readily concede that the evidence presented does not permit a definitive statement regarding mobility processes, it seems apparent from the analysis that the considerable moving about of workers in and out of the labor force (e.g., for purposes of going back to school) or from industry to industry (e.g., for purposes of upgrading through jobhopping) need not translate into substantial improvement. This appears to be particularly true for women and minority workers, who are the most likely to be stuck with the "bad" jobs, although there is some indication that the lack of mobility opportunities is also becoming a problem for white male workers.

The Problem of Transition

The second order of problems is spatial in nature and relates to differences in industrial transformations of places. To state the problem simply, intermetropolitan differences in industrial composition and economic resources give rise to different sets of developmental problems.

From our study of seven places, three patterns seem to emerge, although with considerable overlapping. The first relates to metropolitan economies that have long been dominated by some key manufacturing industries and that have experienced the greatest difficulties in transforming to newer activities. In this study, this pattern of development is exemplified by Buffalo. Such places have been characterized by very slow rates of growth or even by decline, because the long-term stability of their older manufacturing industries has been dramatically threatened by the surge of foreign competition (as in automobiles or chemicals in Buffalo, and also in steel, tires, garments, etc., in other places) and by the competition from relatively cheaper production centers within the United States. While until recently older manufacturing centers such as Buffalo appear to have remained somewhat successful in offering relatively rewarding employment conditions to large segments of the local labor force, they now appear to be under heavy pressure to adjust their earnings distribution structure to compete with cheaper centers. If they do not succeed in making this kind of adjustment, it is probable that decline will continue, with only limited, low paying job openings in sectors such as retail and consumer services taking up some of the slack resulting from lay offs of middle income workers from their older manufacturing base.

The second pattern is found among metropolitan economies in which the distributive, producer, government and nonprofit services have come to play a major role. While not necessarily well equipped to provide for the upward mobility of their workers (with the possible exception of some of the distributive services and certain activities within the public sector), these service industries seem capable of offering reasonably acceptable earnings prospects and employment stability to their employees when compared to other employment sectors. In addition, these are places in which there seem to be a reasonable amount of linkages between the establishments of the large national corporations and the smaller local and regional service- and goods-producing firms. Presumably, these linkages benefit such places because multiplier effects are to a larger extent confined to the locale and because the large firms have a greater, long-term stake in the local economy. Atlanta, Columbus, Nashville, and Charlotte seem to offer several variations of this model.

The third developmental pattern is found among some of the fastest growing places and is exemplified, in this study, by the experience of Phoenix and, to a lesser extent, Denver. In those places, a troublesome paradox seems to be shaping up. While both stand out among the most rapidly growing metropolitan labor markets in the United States, they may also be among the most vulnerable to adverse long-term developments, on at least three grounds.

First, and relative to the other labor markets studied, they tend to have overly developed retail and consumer service sectors that are characterized by poor occupational structures and job laddering. Second, the recent growth of their manufacturing sector has been in industrial areas characterized by highly bifurcated occupational structures (e.g., in electronics). Third, both their manufacturing sector and their corporate headquarters complex seem to stand relatively isolated from the more local or regional part of their economy. In large part, this is because these sectors have become dominated by the presence of the establishments of leading national corporations, which have come in from the outside, have developed only limited linkages to an otherwise underdeveloped structure of small and medium-size local or regional firms, and have remained, thus far, only partially committed to the economic future of the area.*

The implications are at least twofold. The relatively large numbers of "bad jobs" in these economies suggests that avenues for upward mobility are likely to be restricted as too many workers line up for too few opportunities for betterment. In addition, the seemingly heavy dependence of these economies on employment in large firms is such that contraction in some of their key industries may result in substantial lay offs, with few buffer firms to absorb the unemployed. Phoenix appears to have undergone just such an experience in 1975 when unemployment levels rose to 13.2 percent, largely as a result of a sharp contraction in the semiconductor industry. Thus, in several important ways these economies appear to combine some of the worst elements of the current transformation of economic bases. With reduced growth in future years they could easily become the prototype of a developmental scenario that is fraught with labor market difficulties.

The Unstable Dual Economy

The developments adumbrated above suggest that our society may be moving toward an unstable dual economy, in the sense that the transformation of employment systems is pushing toward an increasing separation between two socioeconomic strata with

---

*This lack of linkages to the local economy may not be as serious in Denver as it appears to be in Phoenix.

increasingly restricted bridges between them: a stratum of managers, professionals, technicians, teachers, and other highly skilled employees living in a relatively well protected and well paying economic world, and a large stratum of assembly workers, clericals, and service workers who find it increasingly difficult to make ends meet and to deal with the stress associated with unrewarding and somewhat insecure jobs.

The restrictions faced by workers in the lower strata are multifold and intertwined with one another. Workers must cope with relatively poor earnings and little prospect for improvement in their financial situation, with mostly unskilled jobs offering limited work satisfaction and poor prospects for upgrading, and with jobs whose cyclical and long-term structural security may be highly questionable. The issues of low pay, low skill, and lack of opportunities for upgrading have already been argued at length in this study and need no additional comments. As regards cyclical and long-term employment security, a few tentative observations are warranted. During cyclical downturns, it seems that workers in the lower strata in the services are increasingly becoming the buffer by which employers adjust to contraction, since so much is invested in the higher strata workers, making their lay offs a costly proposition (Berger and Piore, 1980, Chapter 3).

With respect to the long-term structural security of the lower strata jobs, several forces seem at work to undermine it. On the one hand, the security of lower strata employment in the retail and consumer services is partly dependent upon the continued stability of overall per capita consumer income — a trend which has become questionable in the late 1970s and early 1980s — and upon the ability of employees to keep workers' earnings at fairly low levels because of often intense competition in many of these industries (Bailey and Freedman, 1981). If either of these conditions are not met, producers in these service industries may be forced to curtail sharply their activity (to some extent, this is what happened in parts of the retail sectors of older cities, like New York, when the massive exodus of middle-income families to the suburbs shifted a large chunk of the buying power outside the central cities) or to replace more costly service workers by labor-saving technology (not unlike what is happening in the consumer banking area).

On the other hand, the stability of employment in more export-oriented industries (whether in manufacturing or in some of the services) is being challenged by the fact that the footlooseness of many operations of the large corporations is increasing dramatically. Under the pressure of worldwide competition and worldwide reorganization, producing and servicing establishments of the very large firms are becoming increasingly less committed to local economies. They have invested very little in local pools of skilled workers (since they depend mostly on lower-strata workers) and tend to rely increasingly on large multibranch supplier firms (which are themselves becoming highly footloose) rather than on local or regional supplier firms. Thus the continued presence of large semiconductor manufacturers in a place like Phoenix appears to be closely related to a favorable wage structure and an abundant and stable pool of unskilled workers (mostly female and minority workers). If the conditions were to change, one suspects that other locales could quickly offer a replacement site for some of Phoenix's major employers.

Obviously these few statements fall short of exhausting the full complexity of the problems at hand. But perhaps the main findings of the research can easily be summarized in a simple, yet fundamental, observation.

Up to now theorists have viewed segmentation in the labor market in terms of a dualism between the demand that originates from the oligopolistic sector (i.e., large firms) and that which originates from the competitive sector of the economy (i.e., small firms). Within the boundaries of this model, most of the "good" or "medium" jobs are found in the former, while the "bad" jobs are characteristic of the latter. Our research indicates that this picture is rapidly changing. Not only is the importance of "medium" jobs shrinking in relative terms, but oligopolistic sector firms are themselves increasingly characterized by a mix of "good" jobs and "bad" jobs. At a theoretical level, this simply says that a new kind of segmentation has become more important and that the conventional interpretation is becoming more and more out of step with empirical reality.

Policy Recommendations

The danger inherent in the current development toward a society within which two labor markets and, by extension, two societies operate, increasingly divorced from one another, must be reckoned with. Yet not only is this a troublesome development, but the directions needed to bridge the gap between these two societies are not easy to spell out. From the vantage point of the researcher, however, a few suggestions seem warranted.

First, it seems that a strong case can be made for equal employment opportunity programs to pay greater attention to issues of occupational access as opposed to, simply, sex and race discrimination, which is not to suggest that the existing efforts be abandoned.* In addition to helping to correct existing inequities, such a new focus may bring about other positive developments. In those cases where women and minority workers lack the training and education necessary to achieve higher occupational status, such pressure may force employers to think of ways to reorganize internal ladders and to reinstitute intermediate echelons to permit the moving upward of lower-echelon workers.

Still, one should be careful not to think that the solutions to the "truncation" process we are observing will necessarily resemble those of the past. One needs to understand better the ways in which professional and semiprofessional training and licensing may have become an impediment to fluidity in the labor force rather than a means toward amelioration of difficulties. Breaking down some of the barriers they have created may be part of the answer. One also needs to understand better the impact of the new technologies on the occupational structure. It may not be farfetched to argue that the introduction of computer-based technologies has, so far, often been negative from the point of view of the labor market, in that it has tended to further polarize the labor market rather than bridge the gaps. But one has yet to demonstrate the inevitability of this process.

In short, it is very likely that mobility in a service and white collar economy may have to follow a path entirely different from that which existed in a mostly blue collar economy, with the largely free-standing educational system at the center of the new system of mobility. Here one may want to take a closer look at labor market experiences in those countries where employers have at their disposal a more elaborate system of continuing education.

Second, there is a need to identify ways by which greater job security can be reintroduced in the lower occupational segments

---

*For a good review and discussion of the issue, see Blaxall and Reagan (1976).

of labor markets. This requires two things: (1) a better understanding of the ways in which large and very large firms which think "worldwide" may be brought to make a greater commitment to the local economies in which they operate; and (2) a better understanding of the shift that has occurred since the late 1960s among large and small firms in terms of job generation.

The high degree of mobility that nowadays characterizes certain establishments of the large corporation constitutes a serious threat to the long-term viability of the jobs held by many workers in the lower occupational strata. Diminishing the footlooseness of large corporations is, we believe, a key to more stable and more equitable local economic development — if we are to avoid boom town–ghost town phenomena and their social consequences in years to come. Western European countries such as France and Germany have placed much more stringent restrictions on capital mobility and disinvestment for the past two decades, and such restrictions do not appear to have necessarily infringed upon the competitiveness of their industries. Structural adjustments are certainly required in a number of industries, but they are not necessarily incompatible with restrictions on capital mobility. Moreover, because the threat of highly mobile capital is not simply restricted to the older places (Bluestone and Harrison, 1980), we think that carefully thought-out legislation placing some restrictions on capital mobility may be beneficial to both slow *and* fast growing places.

Regarding the shifts in job generation among large and small firms, it is important to note that the 1970s represent a reversal of the trend that characterized the 1960s, during which the share of employment created by large firms grew faster than that created by small firms (Zayas, 1978). We believe that the full implications of this shift have yet to be thought through carefully. Policy thinking around the issue of the rising importance of small firms cannot be reduced either to a fatalistic appraisal regarding the inevitability of small firms in the service industry or to a somewhat uncritical approval of the virtues of small entrepreneurship as the way to industrial rejuvenation. There is every indication that, in labor market terms, small firms, on the whole, can offer only second-best alternatives — and poor ones, at that — to more structured and equitable employment systems (Birch, 1978; Gordon, 1979). Since, in an economy such as ours, a large proportion of the small firms tends to supply goods or services to the large corporations or to government and nonprofit institutions, the rise of small firms may involve largely the shifting of risks from one group of firms to another—whether it be risks involving investment or personnel. There may be a role here for public intervention to ensure that risks do not end up falling largely on workers in the most unsecured occupations.

Third, the issue of increasing duality of earnings cannot be pushed aside indefinitely. While such duality may not yet have translated into a sharp duality in consumer income patterns, since there has been a widespread tendency toward an increase in the number of wage earners within the household, one may worry regarding the desirability of relying on such a remedy. Duality may become rapidly aggravated in a society where traditional household structures are declining and female-headed families and single-individual households are on the rise.

Finally, from the point of view of future policy analysis, further research into the functioning of specific metropolitan labor markets appears to be a fruitful direction in spite of problems with data. Our sense is that some basic improvement in the *Ten Percent Continuous Work History Sample* would provide a promising source of much needed information.

More generally, it seems fair to say that we know very little about current avenues for mobility in a service-oriented economy. These need to be identified more clearly. There is evidence of a major ongoing transformation away from internal labor markets. This issue deserves much more thorough investigation. Lastly, we know very little regarding the role which small and medium-size corporations play in influencing the viability of local economies. Whereas extended linkages between a well-developed network of smaller local or regional firms and large national corporations seem to provide for greater long-term resilience of a local economy, a heavy dependence on job generation in the smaller firms may be questionable in a labor market sense (since most of the jobs they create are among the lowest occupational strata). This seemingly paradoxical situation may be avoided if jobs in the smaller firms are more consciously integrated into the overall mobility structure. Clearly, the sooner the study of these and related issues is begun the better, if policy analysis is to keep abreast of what we see as fundamental changes at work in our society.

Appendices

Appendix Table 1	Classification of Sectors for Gross National Product and Employment Analysis

Agriculture, extractive, and
transformative industries

Agriculture	SIC 01, 02, 07, 08, 09

Extractive and transformative

Mining	SIC 10, 11, 12, 13, 14
Construction	SIC 15, 16, 17
Manufacturing	SIC 20 to 39

Services
  Distributive Services

TCU	SIC 40 to 49
Wholesale	SIC 50, 51

Retail services	SIC 52 to 59

Nonprofit services

Health	SIC 80
Education	SIC 82

Producer services

Finance	SIC 60 to 67
Insurance	
Real estate	
Business services	SIC 73
Legal services	SIC 81
Membership organizations	SIC 86
Miscellaneous professional services	SIC 89
Social services	SIC 83 after 1974

Mainly consumer services

Hotels and other lodging places	SIC 70
Personal services	SIC 72
Auto repair, services and garages	SIC 75
Miscellaneous repair services	SIC 76
Motion pictures	SIC 78
Amusements and recreation services	SIC 79, 84
Private households	SIC 88

Government and government enterprises	SIC 91 to 97

Source: Adapted from J. Singlemann, *From Agriculture to Services* (Beverly Hills, California: Sage Publications, 1978), p. 31.

Appendix 2
Estimation Procedure for Table 4.6

The distribution of employment and average earnings in the combined wholesale-retail category have been disaggregated in Table 4.6 by making use of some of the national averages discussed in Chapter 3 (Tables 3.1, 3.2 and 3.6). For the nation as a whole we observe that 40 percent of the male work force in wholesale-retail combined is employed in wholesale and 60 percent in retail; for female, it is 17 and 83 percent respectively. Assuming that these estimates hold true for the seven SMSA averages for both white male and white female stayers, these proportions are used to disaggregate the stayers work force of both sex groups in Table 4.6.

As we know from Table 4.5 and the discussion presented in Chapter 3, earnings distribution in wholesale resembles more closely that of the TCU sector. We have assumed that the earnings level of white male stayers in wholesale closely approximates that of white male stayers in TCU and have chosen, somewhat arbitrarily, a 1.70 earning index for white male stayers in wholesale (1.79 in TCU). We have then recomputed the earning index for white male stayers in retail so that the figure is internally consistent with our estimate of wholesale earnings and the combined wholesale-retail estimate obtained from the CWHS data. For female stayers, we have used a slightly different method. Females employed in wholesale are overwhelmingly office clericals (Table 3.1 and 3.6). For the nation as a whole, their earnings level was found to be 40 percent above that of all females employed in the retail sector. We have used this figure to estimate earnings levels of white female stayers in wholesale and retail so that, again, these would be consistent with the remaining estimates and with the figures available from the CWHS data.

Appendix Table 3 Distribution of Employment in 1959, 1969, and 1976, and Shares of Job Increases/Job Decreases 1959–1969 and 1969–1976 for Selected Industrial Groupings, United States and Seven SMSAs (in percentages)

UNITED STATES

	1959 Employment	1959–1969		1969 Employment	1969–1976		1976 Employment
		Job increase	Job decrease		Job increase	Job decrease	
Agriculture, extractive, and transformative (total)	38.2	22.7	74.1	33.8	6.7	80.9	28.5
Agriculture	0.2	0.4	0.5	0.3	0.3	–	0.3
Mining	1.3	–	43.6	0.8	1.4	0.4	0.9
Construction	5.0	3.6	–	4.6	2.4	0.6	4.4
Manufacturing	31.7	18.7	30.0	28.1	2.6	79.9	22.9
Services (total)	61.8	77.3	25.9	66.2	93.3	19.1	71.5
Distributive services	11.9	8.0	3.3	10.8	6.8	3.2	10.4
TCU	5.8	4.2	3.3	5.4	2.3	3.2	5.0
Transportation	3.0	2.9	3.0	3.0	1.0	3.2	2.7
Communication	1.7	1.0		1.5	1.0		1.5
Utilities	1.1	0.3		0.9	0.4		0.8
Wholesale	6.1	3.8		5.5	4.5		5.5

Complex of corporate activities	10.3	19.1	21.2	12.7	24.9	2.9	14.7
CAO & A	1.6	4.9		2.5	3.5	0.5	2.7
FIRE	5.0	5.7	2.2	5.1	8.1	2.4	5.7
Banking	1.2	1.8		1.4	2.6		1.6
Insurance	1.5	1.1		1.4	1.0		1.4
Real estate	1.0	0.8		1.0	1.3		1.1
Other fire	1.3	1.9	2.2	1.4	3.2	2.4	1.6
Corporate services	3.6	8.5		5.0	13.2		6.3
Retail services	15.3	14.7	1.3	15.2	19.2	5.9	16.0
Mainly consumer services	4.5	4.1		4.4	4.1	7.1	4.3
Nonprofit	3.5	9.6		5.2	13.1		6.5
Health	2.8	7.1		4.0	11.8		5.3
Education	0.7	2.5		1.2	1.3		1.3
Government	16.3	21.9		17.9	25.3		19.5
Total United States	100.0 (49,638.7)a	100.0 (18,842.3)	100.0 (295.7)	100.0 (68,185.3)	100.0 (11,566.1)	100.0 (2,091.2)	100.0 (77,660.2)
Rates of:							
Job increases		38.0			17.0		
Job decreases			0.6			3.1	
Net employment change			37.4		13.9		

aEmployment in thousands.

(continued on next page)

Appendix Table 3 (continued)

ATLANTA

	1959 Employment	1959–1969		1969 Employment	1969–1976		1976 Employment
		Job increase	Job decrease		Job increase	Job decrease	
Agriculture, extractive, and transformative (total)	32.2	23.8	80.1	28.5	5.1	79.6	20.2
Agriculture	0.3	0.3		0.3	0.2		0.3
Mining	0.2	0.1		0.1		0.2	0.1
Construction	5.5	7.5		6.3	0.4	4.4	5.0
Manufacturing	26.3	16.0	80.1	21.8	4.5	75.1	14.9
Services (total)	67.8	76.2	19.9	71.5	94.9	20.4	79.8
Distributive services	17.0	17.1		17.1	12.7	2.5	16.8
TCU	7.5	8.8		8.1	7.4	2.5	8.2
Transportation	4.4	6.9		5.4	3.6	1.6	5.2
Communication	2.0	1.7		1.9		0.9	1.5
Utilities	1.1	0.3		0.8	3.8		1.5
Wholesale	9.4	8.3		9.0	5.3		8.6

Complex of corporate activities	12.1	20.0	19.9	15.3	35.9	1.9	21.0
CAO & A	1.6	4.7	4.7	2.9	10.1	0.7	4.7
FIRE	6.4	6.8	15.3	6.5	10.5	1.3	7.7
Banking	1.2	2.0		1.5	1.9		1.7
Insurance	2.5	1.6		2.1	1.3		2.0
Real estate	1.0	1.5		1.2	3.5		1.8
Other Fire	1.7	1.8	15.3	1.7	3.8	1.3	2.2
Corporate Services	4.1	8.5		5.9	15.3		8.5
Retail services	15.3	14.2		15.0	16.7	13.0	15.5
Mainly consumer services	5.0	4.4		4.8	7.1	3.0	5.4
Nonprofit	2.9	5.1		3.8	6.6		4.7
Health	1.8	2.7		2.2	6.1		3.3
Education	1.1	2.3		1.6	0.5		1.4
Government	15.5	15.5		15.6	16.0		16.5
Total SMSA	100.0	100.0	100.0	100.0	100.0	100.0	100.0
	(375.5)a	(258.3)	(3.6)	(628.1)	(187.3)	(39.8)	(775.6)
Rates of:							
Job increases	69.1				29.8		
Job decreases						6.3	
Net employment change	68.1		1.0				23.5

a Employment in thousands.

(continued on next page)

Appendix Table 3 (continued)

DENVER-BOULDER

	1959 Employment	1959-1969		1969 Employment	1969-1976		1976 Employment
		Job increase	Job decrease		Job increase	Job decrease	
Agriculture, extractive, and transformative (total)	26.3	21.5	58.2	24.5	19.1	91.1	21.6
Agriculture	0.1	0.3		0.2	0.5		0.3
Mining	0.7	0.9	28.0	0.7	1.4		0.9
Construction	6.3	4.4		5.6	7.3		6.2
Manufacturing	19.3	15.9	30.2	18.0	10.0	91.1	14.2
Services (total)	73.7	78.5	41.8	75.5	80.9	8.9	78.4
Distributive services	16.0	9.3	1.1	13.5	10.5	2.9	12.9
TCU	7.6	4.7	1.1	6.5	4.8	2.9	6.1
Transportation	4.1	3.4	1.1	3.9	2.0	2.9	3.3
Communication	2.4	0.7		1.8	2.1		1.9
Utilities	1.0	0.7		0.9	0.7		0.9
Wholesale	8.4	4.6		7.0	5.7		6.8

Complex of corporate activities	13.0	17.0	40.7	14.5	24.0		17.5
CAO & A	2.1	3.1	13.9	2.5	4.9		3.2
FIRE	6.5	5.9	26.8	6.3	7.8		6.8
Banking	1.2	1.7		1.4	1.9		1.6
Insurance	2.0	1.3		1.7	0.4		1.4
Real estate	1.3	0.8		1.1	2.3		1.5
Other Fire	2.1	2.1	26.8	2.0	3.2		2.4
Corporate Services	4.4	8.0		5.7	11.3		7.5
Retail services	15.8	18.6		16.8	17.6	6.1	17.3
Mainly consumer services	5.2	4.7		5.0	3.7		4.7
Nonprofit	4.7	9.5		6.5	6.3		6.6
Health	3.8	7.3		5.1	6.1		5.5
Education	1.0	2.2		1.4	0.3		1.1
Government	19.0	19.3		19.1	18.7		19.4
Total SMSA	100.0	100.0	100.0	100.0	100.0	100.0	100.0
	(282.3)a	(166.4)	(0.7)	(448.1)	(179.5)	(12.2)	(615.4)
Rates of:							
Job increases	59.0				40.0		
Job decreases			0.2			2.7	
Net employment change		58.8			37.3		

aEmployment in thousands.

(continued on next page)

Appendix Table 3 (continued)

BUFFALO

	1959 Employment	1959–1969		1969 Employment	1969–1976		1976 Employment
		Job increase	Job decrease		Job increase	Job decrease	
Agriculture, extractive, and transformative (total)	46.0	17.5	72.0	39.5	13.1	80.4	31.3
Agriculture	0.1	0.4		0.2			0.1
Mining	0.1	0.1		0.1		0.2	0.1
Construction	4.2	0.7	1.6	3.6	2.1	4.3	3.3
Manufacturing	41.7	16.3	70.4	35.7	11.0	75.7	27.8
Services (total)	54.0	82.5	28.0	60.5	86.9	19.6	68.7
Distributive services	11.3	4.7	9.8	10.0	2.2	6.7	9.8
TCU	5.8	2.7	9.8	5.0	0.9	6.7	4.4
Transportation	3.1	2.7	5.4	3.0	0.9	4.8	2.5
Communication	1.4		3.4	1.1		0.5	1.1
Utilities	1.2		1.0	1.0		1.4	0.8
Wholesale	5.5	2.0		5.0	1.2		5.4

Complex of corporate activities	8.6	19.1	10.1	10.7	24.7	2.5	13.1
CAO & A	1.5	1.3	7.3	1.3	5.3	0.4	1.8
FIRE	3.7	5.3	2.8	4.1	5.9	2.1	4.5
Banking	1.2	1.7		1.3	4.4		1.8
Insurance	1.0	1.9		1.2		1.8	1.0
Real estate	0.6	0.4		0.6	0.1		0.6
Other Fire	0.9	1.3	2.8	0.9	1.3	0.3	1.1
Corporate Services	3.4	12.6		5.3	13.5		6.8
Retail services	14.9	17.1	4.7	15.6	13.3	8.5	16.4
Mainly consumer services	3.6	2.8	3.4	3.5	5.4	2.6	3.9
Nonprofit	3.6	9.0		4.8	20.0		6.9
Health	2.9	8.1		4.0	16.3		5.8
Education	0.7	0.9		0.8	3.7		1.2
Government	11.9	29.9		15.9	21.4		18.6
Total SMSA	100.0	100.0	100.0	100.0	100.0	100.0	100.0
	(404.5)a	(97.4)	(14.9)	(487.0)	(44.3)	(65.4)	(466.0)
Rates of:							
Job increases		24.1			9.1		
Job decreases		3.7			13.4		
Net employment change		20.4			-4.3		

a Employment in thousands.

(continued on next page)

Appendix Table 3 (continued)

PHOENIX

	1959 Employment	1959-1969 Job increase	1959-1969 Job decrease	1969 Employment	1969-1976 Job increase	1969-1976 Job decrease	1976 Employment
Agriculture, extractive, and transformative (total)	28.9	33.0	96.8	29.7	14.1	96.5	22.1
Agriculture	0.3	0.8		0.5	0.3	1.3	0.4
Mining	0.2		2.8	0.1	0.3	0.2	0.1
Construction	9.8	1.9	14.1	5.9	4.9		5.7
Manufacturing	18.7	30.4	79.8	23.2	8.6	95.0	15.8
Services (total)	71.7	67.0	3.2	70.3	85.9	3.5	77.9
Distributive services	14.0	6.8		10.8	9.7	3.1	10.7
TCU	6.3	3.2		4.9	3.4	3.1	4.4
Transportation	2.3	2.0		2.2	1.6	3.1	1.9
Communication	2.4	1.0		1.8	0.9		1.5
Utilities	1.7	0.2		1.0	0.9		1.0
Wholesale	7.6	3.7		5.9	6.3		6.2

Complex of corporate activities	11.1	14.3	3.2	12.8	20.8	0.1	16.0
CAO & A	0.6	1.8	0.8	1.2	3.1		1.9
FIRE	6.7	5.8	2.4	6.4	7.7	0.1	7.0
Banking	1.5	2.2		1.8	1.3		1.7
Insurance	2.0	0.8		1.4	1.5		1.5
Real estate	1.7	1.5		1.6	1.1		1.5
Other Fire	1.6	1.3	2.4	1.4	3.8	0.1	2.3
Corporate Services	3.8	6.7		5.2	9.9		7.0
Retail services	17.6	16.5		17.4	21.2		19.3
Mainly consumer services	7.3	4.9		6.3	5.5	0.3	6.2
Nonprofit	3.2	7.4		5.3	6.6		5.9
Health	2.8	6.1		4.4	6.4		5.3
Education	0.5	1.3		0.9	0.1		0.6
Government	17.9	17.1		17.8	22.2		19.9
Total SMSA	100.0	100.0	100.0	100.0	100.0	100.0	100.0
	(161.3)ª	(146.6)	(5.5)	(302.4)	(149.9)	(14.7)	(437.6)
Rates of:							
Job increases		90.9			49.6		
Job decreases			3.4			4.9	
Net employment change		87.5			44.7		

ªEmployment in thousands.

(continued on next page)

159

Appendix Table 3 (continued)

COLUMBUS

	1959 Employment	1959–1969		1969 Employment	1969–1976		1976 Employment
		Job increase	Job decrease		Job increase	Job decrease	
Agriculture, extractive, and transformative (total)	35.1	22.2	54.5	30.6	7.9	75.8	23.5
Agriculture	0.1	0.2		0.2	0.5		0.2
Mining	0.3		0.5	0.2	0.1		0.2
Construction	4.7	4.2		4.6		6.4	3.7
Manufacturing	30.0	17.8	54.0	25.7	7.2	69.4	19.4
Services (total)	64.9	77.8	45.5	69.4	92.1	24.2	76.5
Distributive services	10.8	6.2	8.5	9.4	8.8	5.1	9.5
TCU	5.0	2.9	8.5	4.3	3.9	5.1	4.1
Transportation	2.5	1.8	8.5	2.1	2.0	3.7	2.0
Communication	1.5	0.8		1.3	1.9		1.5
Utilities	1.0	0.4		0.8		1.3	0.7
Wholesale	5.8	3.3		5.1	4.8		5.4

Complex of corporate activities	12.2	21.3	30.6	14.8	28.0	2.8	18.0
CAO & A	1.7	4.4		2.6	6.4	0.2	3.5
FIRE	5.5	7.9	30.6	5.9	10.2	2.6	6.9
Banking	0.8	1.5		1.1	1.6		1.2
Insurance	1.7	4.0		2.5	4.0		2.9
Real estate	0.9	0.8		0.9	2.4		1.2
Other Fire	2.1	1.5	30.6	1.5	2.2	2.6	1.5
Corporate Services	4.9	9.0		6.3	11.4		7.7
Retail services	15.8	16.3	6.3	16.1	22.2	13.3	17.4
Mainly consumer services	4.1	3.9		4.1	3.4	3.0	4.1
Nonprofit	3.0	6.4		4.1	12.4		5.9
Health	2.5	5.1		3.4	11.6		5.1
Education	0.5	1.3		0.7	0.8		0.8
Government	19.0	23.6		20.8	17.4		21.5
Total SMSA	100.0	100.0	100.0	100.0	100.0	100.0	100.0
	(268.9)a	(125.3)	(6.3)	(388.0)	(81.2)	(28.6)	(440.6)
Rates of:							
Job increases		46.6			20.9		
Job decreases			2.3			7.4	
Net employment change			44.3			13.5	

a Employment in thousands.

(continued on next page)

Appendix Table 3 (continued)

NASHVILLE-DAVIDSON

	1959 Employment	1959–1969		1969 Employment	1969–1976		1976 Employment
		Job increase	Job decrease		Job increase	Job decrease	
Agriculture, extractive, and transformative (total)	35.2	29.6	14.1	33.2	13.4	51.2	28.2
Agriculture	0.2	0.3		0.2	0.4		0.3
Mining	0.3		0.3	0.2	0.1		0.2
Construction	6.2	7.3		6.7	1.7	1.5	5.6
Manufacturing	28.5	22.0	13.9	26.2	11.2	49.7	22.1
Services (total)	64.8	70.4	85.9	65.8	86.6	48.8	71.8
Distributive services	13.2	8.1	4.2	11.3	13.1		12.0
TCU	5.4	3.2	4.2	4.6	7.5		5.4
Transportation	3.0	2.1		2.7	4.2		3.1
Communication	2.1	1.0		1.7	2.8		2.0
Utilities	0.4		4.2	0.2	0.5		0.3
Wholesale	7.7	5.0		6.7	5.6		6.7

Complex of corporate activities	10.7	18.6	81.6	13.2	20.5	5.1	15.1
CAO & A	1.5	5.4		3.0	3.3	1.0	3.1
FIRE	5.9	7.8	81.6	6.1	5.6	4.1	6.0
Banking	1.2	1.8		1.4	2.1		1.6
Insurance	2.0	3.0		2.4	0.7		2.0
Real estate	0.7	0.7		0.7	1.4		0.9
Other Fire	2.1	2.2	81.6	1.6	1.4	4.1	1.5
Corporate Services	3.2	5.4		4.0	11.6		5.9
Retail services	15.1	12.8		14.4	14.3	9.8	14.5
Mainly consumer services	5.2	3.5		4.6	5.4	13.5	4.6
Nonprofit	5.3	9.9		7.1	12.6	20.4	8.0
Health	2.6	5.0		3.5	12.6		5.7
Education	2.7	4.9		3.6		20.4	2.3
Government	15.3	17.5		16.2	20.8		17.7
Total SMSA	100.0	100.0	100.0	100.0	100.0	100.0	100.0
	(163.7)a	(98.0)	(1.8)	(259.9)	(75.9)	(8.4)	(327.4)
Rates of:							
Job increases	59.9				29.2		
Job decreases		1.1				3.2	
Net employment change	58.8				26.0		

a Employment in thousands.

(continued on next page)

163

Appendix Table 3 (continued)

CHARLOTTE-GASTONIA

	1959 Employment	1959-1969 Job increase	1959-1969 Job decrease	1969 Employment	1969-1976 Job increase	1969-1976 Job decrease	1976 Employment
Agriculture, extractive, and transformative (total)	42.3	34.2	52.2	39.2	19.3	75.8	33.5
Agriculture	0.1	0.3		0.2	0.6		0.3
Mining	0.1				0.1		0.1
Construction	7.3	5.4		6.6	7.3		7.0
Manufacturing	34.8	28.5	52.2	32.4	11.3	75.8	26.1
Services (total)	57.7	65.8	47.8	60.8	80.7	24.2	66.5
Distributive services	19.4	15.6		18.0	26.3	6.0	20.3
TCU	8.7	8.5		8.6	19.8	6.0	11.1
Transportation	4.7	6.5		5.4	6.9	6.0	5.7
Communication	1.8	1.4		1.6	0.4		1.4
Utilities	2.2	0.6		1.6	12.5		3.9
Wholesale	10.7	7.1		9.4	6.5		9.2

Complex of corporate activities	9.4	20.6	30.9	13.6	21.7	7.9	15.5
CAO & A	1.5	6.5		3.4	3.6	7.0	3.3
FIRE	5.5	6.1	30.9	5.6	7.9	0.9	6.3
Banking	1.1	2.3		1.6	3.5		2.0
Insurance	2.1	1.1		1.7	1.1		1.7
Real estate	0.8	0.6		0.7	1.2		0.9
Other Fire	1.5	2.0	30.9	1.6	2.1	0.9	1.7
Corporate Services	2.5	8.0		4.6	10.2		5.9
Retail services	13.4	10.8	16.1	12.4	10.3	6.7	12.2
Mainly consumer services	4.7	3.5	0.7	4.3	2.9	3.7	4.0
Nonprofit	2.9	1.9		2.5	6.0		3.4
Health	2.4	1.1		1.9	5.4		2.7
Education	0.5	0.8		0.6	0.6		0.6
Government	7.9	13.4		10.0	13.5		11.1
Total SMSA	100.0 (153.2)a	100.0 (92.8)	100.0 (0.7)	100.0 (245.4)	100.0 (62.2)	100.0 (12.3)	100.0 (295.3)
Rates of:							
Job increases		60.6			25.4		
Job decreases			0.4			5.0	
Net employment change	60.2				20.4		

aEmployment in thousands.

Note: Job increases (decreases) are measured by the net employment gains (losses) in every two-digit SIC industry during each base period (1959–1969 and 1969–1976).

The grouping "Complex of Corporate Activities" includes employment in the Central Administrative Offices and Auxiliary Establishments of Firms (broken down in the *County Business Patterns*) and in producer service firms.

Source: U.S. Bureau of the Census, *County Business Patterns*, 1959, 1969 and 1976, except for government employment which comes from U.S. Bureau of Labor Statistics, *Employment Earnings*. Government employment is not covered by the County Business Patterns.

Appendix Table 4   Distribution of Covered Workforce among Earnings Classes by Industry, for Seven SMSAs, 1975

Earnings Class	Atlanta	Denver	Buffalo	Phoenix	Columbus	Nashville	Charlotte	Modified Average
					Total			
1.60 and above	9.1 (9.1)a	17.3 (17.3)a	0.2	13.2 (10.5)a	9.7 (9.7)a	7.7 (7.7)a	16.0 (16.0)a	9.6
1.20 to 1.59	27.9 (17.3)a (0.6)b (0.8)c	17.7 (12.5)a (0.4)b	42.5 (37.3)a	19.5 (17.0)a (0.1)b	27.9 (21.2)a (1.2)b (0.9)c	25.4 (19.9)a (1.3)b (0.9)c	22.9 (12.3)a (0.6)b (1.3)c	24.7
0.80 to 1.19	19.8 (4.4)b (7.7)c (0.1)d	22.6 (0.5)b (6.3)c (0.1)d	24.5 (2.5)b (13.6)c (0.1)d	29.9 (0.6)b (13.4)c (0.4)d	20.2 (1.3)b (7.0)c (0.5)d	28.2 (2.6)b (9.8)c (2.8)d	21.8 (3.8)b (6.3)c (1.9)d	23.5
0.40 to 0.79	36.7 (0.6)b (6.0)c (4.1)d	36.0 (11.3)c (0.4)d	24.5 (7.0)c (1.6)d	31.9 (4.3)c (0.1)d	35.3 (10.6)c (1.4)d	34.0 (0.3)b (9.7)c (1.2)d	35.1 (0.7)b (10.2)c (2.1)d	34.5
0.39 and below	6.5	6.4	8.3	5.6	6.9	4.7	4.2	6.0

Construction								
1.6 and above	34.2 (34.2)a	64.4 (46.6)a	64.9 (55.8)a	63.3 (48.4)a	70.7 (13.2)a	40.6 (40.6)a	34.5 (34.5)a	53.5
1.20 to 1.59	32.1 (3.9)c (0.7)d	32.4 (1.2)b (4.1)c	13.6 (1.9)b	28.6 (1.2)b (3.2)c	6.0 (2.4)b (3.6)c	33.0 (2.2)c	34.9 (1.9)c	27.9
0.80 to 1.19	30.3 (8.3)b	0.6	18.2 (4.5)c	8.1	22.7	23.1 (3.8)b	28.2 (8.1)b	20.0
0.40 to 0.79	3.4	2.6	3.3		0.6	3.3 (0.5)d	2.4	2.3
0.39 and below								
Manufacturing								
1.60 and above	53.6 (38.3)a	43.0 (43.0)a	63.3 (53.5)a	19.2	55.5 (43.3)a (3.8)b	45.1 (37.5)a	38.9 (31.4)a	47.6
1.20 to 1.59	14.4 (9.5)b	12.1 (1.7)b	27.2 (5.0)b (11.3)c	36.9 (36.9)a	33.5 (15.7)c (2.0)d	10.4 (5.8)b	11.7 (6.3)b	22.2
0.80 to 1.19	31.9 (11.2)c (3.8)d	30.2 (12.1)c (0.4)d	9.5 (1.1)d	27.5 (0.9)b (9.2)c	11.0	44.5 (19.3)c (2.8)d	48.1 (21.3)c (4.7)d	23.7
0.40 to 0.79		14.7		16.4 (0.5)d			1.3	
0.39 and below								

(continued on next page)

Appendix Table 4 (continued)

Earnings Class	Atlanta	Denver	Buffalo	Phoenix	Columbus TCU	Nashville	Charlotte	Modified Average
1.60 and above	49.1 (49.1)a	44.8 (44.8)a	 (55.8)a	48.0 (48.0)a	48.0 (48.0)a	37.4 (37.4)a	46.8 (46.8)a	45.0
1.20 to 1.59	26.9 (8.1)b	10.8 (1.2)b	63.3 (2.2)b	10.2 (1.7)b	26.8 (3.4)b	33.3 (4.9)b	35.2 (5.6)b	26.6
0.80 to 1.19	15.2 (11.0)c	36.4 (17.9)c	24.3 (15.5)c	30.5 (19.2)c	12.6 (14.9)c	13.8 (17.9)c	14.6 (13.3)c	19.7
0.40 to 0.79	7.4 (1.7)d	8.0 (1.2)d	12.4 (1.3)d	11.3 (1.1)d	12.6 (2.9)d	15.5 (2.4)d	3.4 (1.7)d	10.3
0.39 and below	1.4							

Wholesale/Retail

1.60 and above	35.0 (25.0)a	26.3 (26.3)a	25.2 (25.2)a	25.4 (25.4)a	25.7 (25.7)a	26.0 (26.0)a	26.9 (26.9)a	25.7
1.20 to 1.59	9.5 (4.9)b	15.1 (0.7)b	10.4 (0.8)b	17.0 (0.5)b	12.8 (1.7)b	15.9 (3.5)b	11.6	12.9
0.80 to 1.19	41.2 (13.4)c (2.7)d	40.7 (16.5)c (0.4)d	30.6 (22.5)c (0.8)d	40.5 (13.9)c (0.2)d	41.7 (18.0)c (1.2)d	40.7 (17.5)c (1.6)d	10.2 (4.5)b	40.1
0.40 to 0.79	14.3	17.9	33.9	17.1	19.8	17.4	37.3 (15.3)c (2.3)d	17.3
0.39 and below			4.1				14.0	
FIRE								
1.60 and above	21.5 (21.5)a	20.3 (20.3)a	26.3 (26.3)a	20.8 (20.8)a	24.7 (24.7)a	21.2 (21.2)a	25.0 (25.0)a	21.6
1.20 to 1.59	12.5	7.2	7.7 (1.0)b	9.3	6.0	11.2	9.7	10.0
0.80 to 1.19	30.9 (2.8)b (21.0)c	39.7 (0.3)b (26.1)c (0.6)d	61.9 (32.5)c (2.1)d	35.4 (0.4)b (19.0)c	39.9 (2.1)b (28.6)c	37.6 (2.4)b (25.3)c (2.4)d	33.1 (3.2)b (20.2)c	35.3
0.40 to 0.79	35.1	32.8		34.1	29.3	30.0	32.2	32.8
0.39 and below	(4.0)d			0.4	(2.1)d		(2.4)d	

(continued on next page)

Appendix Table 4 (continued)

Earnings Class	Atlanta	Denver	Buffalo	Phoenix	Columbus (Other services)	Nashville	Charlotte	Modified Average
1.60 and above	12.6 (12.6)[a]	17.2 (17.2)[a]		18.2 (18.2)[a]	18.9 (18.9)[a]	15.6 (15.6)[a]	14.7 (14.7)[a]	15.7
1.20 to 1.59	5.5		23.4 (20.0)[a]			3.7 (3.7)[b]	6.5	3.1
0.80 to 1.19	28.0 (3.1)[b] (21.0)[c]	12.4 (0.7)[b]	38.3 (1.1)[b] (33.6)[c]	41.7 (0.4)[b] (27.8)[c] (0.9)[d]	12.2 (1.8)[b]	55.9 (28.3)[c] (9.0)[d]	45.9 (2.9)[b] (24.5)[c] (8.4)[d]	33.3
0.40 to 0.79	45.9 (8.0)[d]	68.6 (24.9)[c] (1.2)[d]	37.1 (3.4)[d]	39.2	64.4 (22.3)[c] (3.4)[d]	24.8	32.9	43.9
0.39 and below	8.0	1.8	1.2	0.9	4.5			1.7

[a]White male stayers, same industries; [b]Black male stayers, same industries; [c]White female stayers, same industries; [d]Black female stayers, same industries.

Note: The distributions presented in this appendix table are not true distributions of workers among earnings classes. Rather they represent the result of distributing each sex-race flow of workers according to its earnings class (see Chapter 3). For each industry there are four flows (stayers, job inmovers, new entrants and immigrants) times six sex-race groups, that is, a total of twenty-four cells to be distributed. Only the average earnings of all workers in each cell is known. The share of employment in each of the four stayers cells in every industry is indicated in parentheses to provide additional detail.

Source: U.S. Bureau of Economic Analysis, *Ten Percent Continuous Work History Sample.*

Bibliography

Abramovitz, Moses. "Manpower, Capital and Technology." In *Human Resources and Economic Welfare, Essays in Honor of Eli Ginzberg,* edited by Ivar Berg. New York: Columbia University Press, 1972.

Bailey, Thomas, and Marcia Freedman. "Immigrants and Native-Born Workers in the Restaurant Industry." Mimeographed. New York: Conservation of Human Resources, 1981.

Berger, Suzanne, and Michael J. Piore. *Dualism and Discontinuity in Industrial Societies.* New York: Cambridge University Press, 1980.

Birch, David. "Statement to the Committee on Small Business" in U.S. House of Representatives, *Hearings on Small Business and Job Creation.* Washington, D.C.: G.P.O., 1978. Pp. 36–63.

Blaxall, Martha, and Barbara Reagan, eds. *Women and the Workplace: The Implications of Occupational Segregation.* Chicago: University of Chicago Press, 1976.

Bluestone, Barry, and Bennett Harrison. *Capital and Communities: The Causes and Consequences of Private Disinvestment.* Washington, D.C.: The Progressive Alliance, 1980.

Brecher, Charles. *Upgrading Blue Collar and Service Workers.* Baltimore: The Johns Hopkins University Press, 1972.

Chandler, Alfred J. *The Visible Hand: The Managerial Revolution in American Business.* Cambridge: Harvard University Press, 1977.

Cohen, Robert. "The Internationalization of Capital and U.S. Cities." Ph.D. dissertation, New School for Social Research, 1977.

171

Colorado Energy Research Institute. *Impacts of Energy Resource Development on the Denver Metropolitan Area*. Golden, Colorado, June 1979.

Conservation of Human Resources Project. *The Corporate Headquarters Complex in New York City*. New York: December 1977.

Denison, Edward. *Accounting for Slower Economic Growth: The U.S. in the 1970s*. Washington, D.C.: Brookings Institution, 1979.

Doeringer, Peter, and Michael J. Piore. *Internal Labor Markets and Manpower Analysis*. Lexington, Mass.: D.C. Heath Lexington Books, 1971.

Dun and Bradstreet. *Million Dollar Directory*. New York: McGraw-Hill, 1976.

Dunn, Edgar S., Jr. *The Development of the U.S. Urban System*. Baltimore: The Johns Hopkins University Press, 1980.

Fortune Magazine. *1961 Plant and Product Directory of the 500 Largest U.S. Industrial Corporations*. New York: Time, Inc., 1961.

Freedman, Marcia. *Labor Markets: Segments and Shelter*. Montclair, N.J.: Allanheld, Osmun, 1976.

Gordon, David M. *The Working Poor: Towards a State Agenda*. Washington, D.C.: The Council of State Planning Agencies, 1979.

Hiestand, Dale L., and Dean Morse. *Comparative Metropolitan Employment Complexes: New York, Chicago, Los Angeles, Houston, Atlanta*. Montclair, N.J.: Allanheld, Osmun, 1979.

Marketing Economics Institute. *1975–76 Key Plants Directory*. New York: Marketing Economics Institute, 1976.

Myers, John. "GNP: Perspectives on Services." Mimeographed. New York: Conservation of Human Resources, 1980.

National Register. *Directory of Corporate Affiliations*. Skokie, Ill.: National Register Publishing Co., 1976.

Noyelle, Thierry J., and Thomas M. Stanback, Jr. *Economic Transformation in American Cities*, forthcoming.

Pred, Allan. *City Systems in Advanced Economies*. New York: John Wiley & Sons, 1977.

Singlemann, J. *From Agriculture to Services*. Sage Library of Social Research, Vol. 69. Beverly Hills: Sage Publications, 1978.

Stanback, Thomas, Jr. *Understanding the Service Economy*. Baltimore: The Johns Hopkins University Press, 1979.

Stanback, Thomas, Jr., Peter J. Bearse, Thierry J. Noyelle, and Robert A. Karasek. *Services/The New Economy*. Totowa, N.J.: Allanheld, Osmun, 1981.

Stanback, Thomas M., Jr., and Richard V. Knight. *Metropolitan Economy*. New York: Columbia University Press, 1970.

Thompson, Wilbur R. "The Economic Base of Urban Problems." In *Contemporary Economic Issues*, edited by Neil W. Chamberlain. Homewood, Illinois: Richard D. Irwin, 1969.

U.S. Bureau of the Census. *County Business Patterns*. Washington, D.C.: U.S. Department of Commerce, 1959, 1969, 1976.

U.S. Bureau of the Census. *Statistical Abstract of the United States*. Washington, D.C.: U.S. Department of Commerce, 1979, 1980.

U.S. Bureau of the Census. *Survey of Income and Education*. Washington, D.C.: U.S. Department of Commerce, 1976.

U.S. Bureau of Economic Analysis. *The National and Product Account of the United States, 1929-74*. Washington, D.C.: U.S. Department of Commerce, 1977.

U.S. Bureau of Economic Analysis. *Ten Percent Continuous Work History Sample of the Social Security Administration*. Washington, D.C.: U.S. Department of Commerce, 1971, 1973, 1975.

U.S. Bureau of Economic Analysis. "U.S. National Income and Product Accounts: Revised Estimates, 1975-77." In *Survey of Current Business*, July 1978. Washington, D.C.: U.S. Department of Commerce, 1978.

U.S. Bureau of Labor Statistics. *Employment and Earnings*. Washington, D.C.: U.S. Department of Labor, 1959, 1969, 1976.

U.S. Bureau of Labor Statistics. *Tomorrow's Manpower Needs, National Industry-Occupational Matrix*. Washington, D.C.: U.S. Department of Labor, Microdata, 1960, 1967, 1970, 1976.

U.S. House of Representatives. Committee on Small Business, *Hearings on Small Business and Job Creation*. 95th Congress. Washington, D.C.: U.S. Government Printing Office, 1978.

Zayas, Edison R. "Statement to the Committee on Small Business," in U.S. House of Representatives, *Hearings on Small Business and Job Creation*. Washington, D.C.: G.P.O., 1978. Pp. 106-34.

Index

175

Thomas M. Stanback, Jr., is Professor of Economics at New York University and Senior Research Associate at the Conservation of Human Resources Project, Columbia University. He is the author of *Understanding the Service Economy* and coauthor of *Electronic Data Processing in New York City, The Metropolitan Economy: The Process of Employment Expansion, Suburbanization and the City,* and *Services/The New Economy.*

Thierry J. Noyelle is Research Associate at the Conservation of Human Resources Project, Columbia University. He has published articles in the areas of urban and regional development, economic planning, and labor market segmentation. He is coauthor of *Services/The New Economy.*